The Hiking Trails of Florida's National Forests, Parks, and Preserves, Second Edition

D0368563

UNIVERSITY PRESS OF FLORIDA

Florida A&M University, Tallahassee
Florida Atlantic University, Boca Raton
Florida Gulf Coast University, Ft. Myers
Florida International University, Miami
Florida State University, Tallahassee
University of Central Florida, Orlando
University of Florida, Gainesville
University of North Florida, Jacksonville
University of South Florida, Tampa
University of West Florida, Pensacola

The Hiking Trails of Florida's National Forests, Parks, and Preserves SECOND EDITION

Johnny Molloy and Sandra Friend

University Press of Florida
Gainesville · Tallahassee · Tampa · Boca Raton
Pensacola · Orlando · Miami · Jacksonville · Ft. Myers

This book is still for Meredith.

Copyright 2007 by Johnny Molloy and Sandra Friend
Printed in the United States of America on acid-free paper

12 11 10 09 08 07   6 5 4 3 2 1

Library of Congress Cataloging-in-Publication Data

Molloy, Johnny, 1961–
The hiking trails of Florida's national forests, parks, and preserves /
Johnny Molloy and Sandra Friend.—2nd ed.
p. cm.
ISBN 978-0-8130-3062-3 (alk. paper)
1. Hiking—Florida—Guidebooks. 2. Trails—Florida—Guidebooks.
3. National parks and reserves—Florida—Guidebooks. 4. Florida—
Guidebooks. I. Friend, Sandra. II. Title.
GV199.42.F6M65 2007
796.5209759—dc22   2007001294

The University Press of Florida is the scholarly publishing agency for the State
University System of Florida, comprising Florida A&M University, Florida Atlantic
University, Florida Gulf Coast University, Florida International University, Florida
State University, University of Central Florida, University of Florida, University of
North Florida, University of South Florida, and University of West Florida.

University Press of Florida
15 Northwest 15th Street
Gainesville, FL 32611-2079
http://www.upf.com

Contents

Preface

The first hike I took in Florida was in the Bradwell Bay Wilderness of the Apalachicola National Forest, but the story actually starts in the Smoky Mountains near my Tennessee home. There I cut my hiking teeth, starting with summer day hikes and short overnight backpacks. As the desire to see what was around the corner increased, hiking and backpacking adventures extended into spring and fall. The natural evolution of this trend was to head into the mountains during winter. Winter hiking and camping in the Smokies can be a challenge. By this time my camping frequency was up to a hundred nights or more per year. Numerous winter trips in a row can be more than even the most enthusiastic hiker can stand. Thus began my quest to find a warmer place to hike during the winter months.

I grabbed an atlas and looked south on the map. To my surprise there were three large green spots, indicating national forests in Florida. I made plans and soon made that first trip to Bradwell Bay Wilderness, hiking the Florida Trail. What an enlightening event—the beauty was evident from the initial step. I returned to the Apalachicola on a regular basis, both hiking and canoeing. Finding other wild slices of the Florida landscape, such as the Everglades backcountry and the beaches of St. Joseph Peninsula, changed my view of the state forever.

In due course I became an outdoor writer, turning my passion for wild places into a vocation. My first writing venture in the Sunshine State was *The Best in Tent Camping: Florida*. I learned much more about the natural landscape, from Gulf Islands National Seashore in the northwest to Bahia Honda State Park in the southeast. I found miles upon miles of trails to hike. Seemingly everywhere the Florida National Scenic Trail cropped up.

After this, I wrote *Beach and Coastal Camping in Florida*, which reinforced my realization of what a fantastic natural resource Florida is. While researching these books, I took side trips, from short day hikes to multinight adventures. My next Florida writing experience was penning *A Paddlers Guide to Everglades National Park*. By this time I was spending every winter exploring the Florida outdoors. Next came the first edition of this book.

With a fairly good knowledge base, I set forth to hike all the trails described in this guidebook. While hiking these trails I learned that I had much more to learn and discover. And what a pleasure it was—walking the sand pine hills of the Juniper Prairie Wilderness, watching the sun set while camped on a tropical tree island in the Big Cypress National Preserve, looking over the Atlantic Ocean from Elliott Key and treading the ground at Olustee Battlefield, site of Florida's largest Civil War engagement.

Sure there were bad times—lying under a four-by-six-foot tarp with two other backpackers while a terrible storm raged around us, complete with tornadoes; getting eaten up by mosquitoes on the Bear Lake Trail; trying to type up trail descriptions with frozen fingers near Ocean Pond while it was 25 degrees outside the tent. But these inconveniences were the spices in the entrée—the experience in totality was a joy.

Possibly the most memorable experiences of all were meeting the many fine folks along the way; the volunteers at the Florida Trail Association, the national forest and park staff, and other hikers who shared my passion for the hiking trails of Florida's national forests, parks, and preserves.

After the first edition of this book, I paddled the length of Florida and wrote an adventure story about it, *From the Swamp to the Keys: A Paddle through Florida History*. This book wove together Florida's past and present, deepening my understanding of the state. The response to the book was good. In 2006 I through-hiked the Florida Trail, writing another adventure story titled *Adventures on the Florida Trail: An 1,100 Mile Walk through the Sunshine State*. The Florida Trail serves as the backbone to the state's wild hiking lands, connecting the disparate hiking areas profiled in the present book. The experience was memorable and reinforced what a great hiking destination Florida is.

Working on the second edition has been reinforcing as well. And with Sandra Friend's hiking expertise, the revised edition is not only new but improved. May this book help you go out and make some Florida outdoor memories of your own.

Acknowledgments

From Johnny: Thanks to David Stenger for giving me a ride in the Ocala; David Carroll for running shuttle in the Ocala; Chris Phillips for hiking, camping, and running shuttle in the Ocala and Apalachicola; Bernadette

Pedagano for running shuttle and camping with me; Jason Money at Long Pine Key Campground; and Tim Downey, Roy Wood, and John and Barb Haapala at Everglades National Park. Thanks also to John Cox for hiking with me at Big Cypress; Kent Wimmer at the Florida Trail office in Tallahassee; Ron Traylor, Meredith, Ken, and Aaron Marable for running shuttle in the Apalachicola; Nina Dupuy for information about Big Cypress; Francisco Meyer, Laura Young, Nelson Martin at Sopchoppy Outfitters, Tom Lauria, Debbie Lauria, Tina Dean, and Robert Seidler. And thanks to David Haynes, Nate Carbaugh, Kent Dumont, Mark Williams, Nicole Gordon, Hunt Cochrane, and Tom Rodgers.

From Sandra: Thanks to my husband Rob Smith Jr. for enjoying the wilds of the Apalachicola and Osceola national forests with me; to Janet Chernoff, for arranging our Wakulla Lodge stay; to Pat Villenueve and Tom Daly for joining us at Leon Sinks; to Dan, Terri, Shania and Yosef Singer, my Everglades aficionados; to Kathy Wolf, for Kathy's B&B; to Michelle Mitchell, Denise Rains, Terry Tenold, Susan Kett, and Marsha Kearney for assistance on research in the national forests in Florida; to Bob Coveney, Deborah Stewart-Kent, Deb Blick, Bob Woods, and "Chicken" Dave Fevier for adventures on the Western Connector; and to my dear friend Phyllis "Shortcut" Malinski, who will finish hiking the entire Florida Trail before I do. Phyllis, this one is for you.

Introduction

Welcome to the second edition of this book. As we all know, the landscape of Florida can, will, and does change, whether from the human hand or the wrath of nature. And trails change along with it. Documenting these changes, including the time spent hiking, can be daunting. As an outdoor enthusiast and hiking expert I wanted to get it right for readers and aspiring outdoor fans who want to explore Florida's unique places on foot. To that end I recruited Florida hiking legend Sandra Friend, who grew up in the mountains of New Jersey and moved to Florida as a teen. She has been walking Florida's footpaths since the 1970s and has hiked over 2,200 miles of these trails since 2001, the year she bought the first edition of this book. Now she works for the Florida Trail Association and is a key player in the Sunshine State hiking community. Sandra has contributed immensely to the second edition, making this book much better.

Over time, some trails have grown longer and more interesting, and some trails have disappeared altogether. We found instances of both. The Florida Trail through the Ocala National Forest has added a Western Connector, which meets the Eastern Corridor near Lake Kerr. However, hurricanes have completely altered the Florida Trail at Gulf Islands National Seashore and closed the Eco Pond Loop at Everglades National Park.

In the first edition (2001) I mentioned hiking trails in Florida not receiving the acclaim of other destinations. Times have changed. The development and evolution of the master path of the state, the Florida Trail, and further development of other paths by the Florida Trail Association and other public entities are bringing attention to the quality hiking throughout the Sunshine State. Before, during, and after my through-hike of the Florida Trail in 2006, I was surprised at how many people in the hiking world beyond the state borders, as well as those within, had hiked on or heard of the Florida Trail.

And as more and more transplants move here from other states, bringing with them their passion for hiking, they find surprisingly ample outlets for restless feet and pass on the word about just how good the hiking in Florida can be. What makes hiking here so appealing?

A unique hiking environment is one key ingredient—most of Florida stretches along a peninsula that juts southward into Atlantic Ocean and Gulf of Mexico. Florida's place on the North American continent results in the state having flora unlike that of other hiking areas in the United States. Where else on U.S. mainland can you walk beneath tall palms or tread through a tropical hardwood hammock?

Florida has a long hiking season and is ideal for walking during times when it can be unpleasant elsewhere. In the lower part of the peninsula, in such areas as Everglades National Park, the drier, cooler weather is during winter and early spring. In Central Florida the hiking season extends from late fall through early spring. Finally, moving north, hikers can comfortably enjoy the trails from fall through spring.

There is more to the landscape than appears at first glance. Many would describe the terrain here as flat. However, in Florida small changes in elevation make big differences. A matter a few feet can result in wildly different habitats, as surely as thousands of feet change habitats in the Rocky Mountains. A small hill in Florida may harbor pine woods, then a nearly imperceptible depression leads to a lush subtropical swamp. Water is a major element of most Florida hiking experiences, whether one is walking through a subtropical swamp, or alongside a spring fed pond, or crossing a blackwater creek. The locals know, and the newcomers are finding out; armed with this book, anyone can discover what makes hiking in Florida unique.

Clothing

Hiking in Florida requires more clothing for different reasons than one might suppose. Major concerns are rain, sun, insects, and cold. Yes, cold. For cold does happen in Florida, from the Panhandle to the Everglades. When the north winds blow, add clothing in layers—a light wool sweater and/or some type of synthetic apparel in addition to the layer next to your skin. This way you can adjust your clothing with changes in temperature. For rain, carry a poncho at minimum. A poncho can be a good choice, as it is not as stifling as a full rain jacket or rain suit, inside which heat will build.

Sun is a major consideration. Many hiking areas are open to the sky, and the sun can beat down and burn the unprepared. A shade-producing hat, long-sleeved shirt, and long pants will keep potentially damaging sun off you. A neckerchief and sunscreen will protect you further. The very same clothing items that screen you from Sol will also keep the bugs at bay, for clothes are the best protection against the "swamp angels" and no-see-ums and other little pests. In tick country, tuck your pant legs into your socks to keep these hangers-on from hitching a ride and then a meal off you.

Footwear is another concern. Though sandals or tennis shoes may seem the logical choice, many Florida trails are muddy and uneven and sometimes even rocky. Tennis shoes may not offer enough support. Sport sandals leave much of your foot exposed. Mosquito-bitten ankles or a sliced foot far from the trailhead will make for a miserable limp back to the car. Lightweight boots and heavyweight running shoes are the footwear of choice. I prefer lightweight hiking boots with a minimum of leather; this way the boots dry out faster. Boots should have ankle support but not be so high that heat can't escape. For day hiking, Sandra prefers running shoes. They wick off sweat and dry out quickly when you hike in soggy places, and they provide good traction on sand.

Safety Concerns

To some outdoor enthusiasts, the forests and swamps of Florida seem laden with hazards—snakes, bears, and alligators. It is the fear of the unknown that causes this anxiety. Potentially dangerous situations can occur in the outdoors, just as they can occur where you live, but as long as you use sound judgment and prepare yourself before you hit the trail, you'll be much safer in the woods than in most urban areas of the country. It is better to view a backcountry hike as a fascinating discovery of the unknown than as a potential setting for disaster. Here are a few tips to make your trip safer and easier:

Always bring food and water, whether you are going overnight or not. Food will give you energy, will help keep you warm, and may sustain you in an emergency situation until help arrives. And you never know

Figure 1. A tent with bugproof mesh or insect netting is a must for Florida backcountry campers. Photo by Johnny Molloy

whether you will have a stream or swamp nearby when you become thirsty. Treat water before drinking from a stream. The likelihood of getting sick from the organism known as giardia or some other waterborne organism is small, but there is no reason to take a chance. Boil or filter all water before drinking it. If you are staying out overnight, some kind of shelter and insect netting are a must. It takes only a few swamp angels to ruin a good night's sleep.

Stay on designated trails. The way hikers get lost is usually by leaving the path. If you become disoriented, don't panic—that may result in a bad decision that will make your predicament worse. The flatwoods and wetlands of Florida offer few high points from which to orient yourself. Retrace your steps if you can, or stay put. Rangers check the trails first when searching for lost or overdue hikers.

Bring a map, compass, and lighter, and know how to use a map and compass. Should you get lost, these three items can help you stick around long enough to be found or get yourself out of a pickle. Trail maps are available at ranger stations or visitor centers. A compass can help you orient yourself, and a lighter can start a fire for signaling or warmth. Be especially careful when crossing streams and swamps. Whether you are fording or crossing on a footlog, make every step count. When fording a stream, use a stout limb as a third leg for balance. Many Florida streams are tannic black water, and the bottom can't be seen—feel ahead with each foot, making sure to gain purchase with every step.

Be aware of the symptoms of hypothermia—even in Florida. Shivering and forgetfulness are the two most common indicators of this cold-weather killer. Hypothermia can occur when the temperature is in the 50s, especially when a wet hiker is wearing lightweight cotton clothing. If symptoms arise, get the victim shelter, hot liquids, and dry clothes or a dry sleeping bag.

Always bring rain gear. Thunderstorms can come on suddenly in the summer, and winter fronts can soak you to the bone. Keep in mind that a rainy day is as much a part of nature as those idyllic ones you desire. Rainy days really cut down on the crowds—a normally crowded trail can be a place of solitude for those with appropriate rain gear. Do remember that getting wet opens the door to hypothermia.

Take along your brain. A cool, calculating mind is the single most important piece of equipment you'll ever need on the trail. Think before you act. Watch your step. Plan ahead. Avoiding accidents before they happen is the best recipe for a rewarding, stress-relieving hike. Use your head out there, and treat the place like a careful and respectful owner would. After all, the national forests, parks, and preserves belong to us all.

Tips for Enjoying the Trails of Florida

Before you head to your chosen destination, order a map or information kit. The phone numbers and Web sites for each place can be found in the information section at the back of the book. This information will help you get oriented to the roads, features, and attractions of Florida's wild places. The following tips will make your visit enjoyable and rewarding:

Investigate different areas of the state. Biscayne National Park has tropical forests and ocean views. The Everglades offer unique habitats seen nowhere else on earth. The Ocala National Forest has sand pine scrub forests and spring-fed lakes. Osceola National Forest has gum swamps and extensive pine flatwoods. Apalachicola National Forest has big rivers and the Bradwell Bay Wilderness. Big Cypress has dwarf bald cypress forests and tropical tree islands. A mosaic of habitats covers the entirety of Florida. The biodiversity of the state is truly amazing.

Take your time along the trails. Pace yourself. Florida's national forests, parks, and preserves are filled with wonders both big and small. Examine the minnows in the limestone solution holes of Big Pine Key. Grab a wide view of Turtle Mound at Canaveral National Seashore. Watch the sun set on Hopkins Prairie. Smell the slash pine woods on the tree islands of the Big Cypress. See a deer disappear into a palmetto thicket near Olustee Battlefield. Check out the riot of titi blooms along a wetland near Camel Lake.

Pick your times well. When possible, try to hike during the week and avoid the traditional holidays. If you are hiking on busy days, go early in the morning; it will enhance your chances of seeing wildlife, besides beating the crowd.

Weather

Florida's climate attracts outdoor enthusiasts year-round. But the weather here cannot be summed up easily—the state is spread over such a large area. To understand the climate better, we need to Florida divide into three areas: north, central, and south.

North Florida covers the area from Pensacola to Jacksonville. The hiking season here generally lasts from fall through spring. This area of the state lies on the south side of the continental mainland and in the upper part of the Florida peninsula. There are four distinct seasons here, though the climate is very long on summer, when highs regularly reach the 90s and a thunderstorm can come on almost any afternoon. Nights can be uncomfortably hot. Fall finds cooler nights and warm days, with less precipitation than in summer.

Winter is variable. Highs push 65 degrees. Expect lows in the 40s, though subfreezing temperatures are the norm during cold snaps. There are usually several mild days during each winter month. Precipitation comes in strong continental fronts, with more persistent rains followed by cold, sunny days. Snow is uncommon, though not unheard of. The longer days of spring begin to warm up, even becoming hot, but this season can vary wildly.

Central Florida covers the portion of the peninsula from Gainesville south to the north shore of Lake Okeechobee. The hiking season here runs from late fall through spring. Winter is generally pleasant and dry. Daytime highs reach and often surpass 70 degrees, yet the area is far enough north for a cold snap to bring afternoon highs down to the 50s and occasional temperatures below freezing.

Spring is a welcome season. The days are warm and clear, often topping 80 degrees, yet nights remain cool enough to put on a long-sleeved shirt or sweater. Mornings are often still crisp. Beginning around May, the days really warm up. Moist air drifts in from the Gulf and thunderstorms regularly result. Daytime highs often exceed 90 degrees during the long, humid summer. Late fall can be very nice. The thunderstorms have subsided and cool fronts clear the skies.

South Florida lies from Lake Okeechobee southward to Key West. The hiking season in the deep south of the state normally spans winter and early spring. Here, the coastal reaches are influenced by their proximity to ocean waters, which moderate temperatures. The center of the peninsula has more extreme temperatures, both hot and cold. Though South Florida is in the humid tropical climate zone, winter cold fronts occasionally make their way this far down. Short periods of rain are normally followed by several clear, dry days with highs in the low to mid-70s. Pleasant nights can cool off to the low 50s.

The dry season, as much of winter is known here, lasts from December through April. This is when the snowbirds flock south. As summer thunderstorms increase in frequency, so do the insects. The interior of South Florida can become oppressively hot, but ocean breezes occasionally make coastline conditions more tolerable. As summer gives way to fall, the likelihood of a hurricane is a distinct possibility. Temperatures come down a bit, but high rainfall happens with regularity.

How to Use This Guidebook

Opening the section on each hike is a block of information that allows the hiker quick access to pertinent details: where the trail begins and ends, distance, trail condition, highlights, hazards, trail connections, hiking season, maps, and trailhead directions (SR = state road, CR = county road, FR = forest road). An example follows:

Salt Springs Spur Trail

Begin: Salt Springs Marina Road
End: Florida Trail, northwest of Hopkins Prairie
Distance: 2.7 miles
Trail Difficulty: Moderate
Highlights: Ponds and prairies
Hazards: Some sun exposure
Trail Connections: Florida Trail, Hopkins Prairie to Salt Springs Island
Season: Late fall–spring
Maps: Ocala National Forest map
Trailhead: From Ocala, drive east on SR 40 for 12 miles, then turn left on CR 314 and follow it for 18 miles to SR 19. Turn left on SR 19 and follow it 0.1 mile to Salt Springs Marina Road, FR 22. Turn right on FR 22 and follow it 100 yards to the trailhead on your right.

Thus much of the critical information is in the opening summary. This hike starts at Salt Springs Marina Road and ends at the Florida Trail northwest of Hopkins Prairie. It is 2.7 miles long and trail difficulty is moderate. On the way you will see prairies and ponds. Some sections of the trail are exposed to the sun. The trail connects to the Hopkins Prairie to Salt Springs Island section of the Florida Trail. The best hiking season is from late fall through spring. The Maps section tells you which map covers this trail. Directions to the trailhead are included.

Following each block is a running narrative of the hike, a detailed account in which trail junctions, stream crossings, and trailside features are noted along with their distance from the trailhead. This helps keep you apprised of your whereabouts as well as making sure you don't miss the features noted. You can use this guidebook to walk just a portion of a trail or combine the trail information to plan a hike of your own.

Obtaining Maps

Hikers will want a map, if available. The best source for this is the overall park and forest maps. Other trails and trail areas have their own maps. If so, this is indicated in the each trail's information box. These handouts can be obtained at ranger stations and visitor centers. Some trails, including many national forest trails, have maps posted on the Internet. For some trails, especially the interpretive trails, there is no map. However, the information included for each hike will get you to the trailhead and on the pathway of your choice. Check the area you plan to hike, visit the Web site if there is one, or call the contact number to obtain a map.

Biscayne National Park
www.nps.gov/bisc
(305) 230-7275

Ocala National Forest
www.fs.fed.us/r8/florida/
(352) 669-3153

Everglades National Park
www.nps.gov/ever
(305) 242-7700

Osceola National Forest
www.fs.fed.us/r8/florida/
(904) 752-2577

Big Cypress National Preserve
www.nps.gov/bicy
(941) 695-4111

Apalachicola National Forest
http://www.fs.fed.us/r8/florida/
(850) 643-2282

Canaveral National Seashore
www.nps.gov/cana
(386) 428-3384

Gulf Islands National Seashore
www.nps.gov/guis
(850) 934-2600

The trails have been arranged within the eight areas they cover: Biscayne and Everglades national parks, Big Cypress National Preserve, Canaveral National Seashore, the Ocala, Osceola, and Apalachicola national forests, and Gulf Islands National Seashore. Flip thorough the book and find the hikes most appealing to you, then get out there and hit the trail!

Osceola National Forest

Canaveral
National
Seashore

Gulf Islands
National Seashore

Apalachicola
National Forest

Ocala National Forest

Big Cypress National Preserve

Everglades National Park

Biscayne National Park

Hiking Trails of Biscayne National Park

Biscayne National Park is the most watery preserve in the entire national park system, 93 percent submerged. Known for these crystal clear waters and attendant activities such as snorkeling, fishing, and boating, it also has trails.

Located in the Atlantic Ocean southeast of Miami, Biscayne is accessible only by boat. Most visitors come in their private craft; however, there is a ferry run by a park concessionaire, starting at Convoy Point, the park's mainland headquarters. Once on the islands you can step back into a history that extends back thousands of years. These keys were first an Indian stronghold. Later, white settlers farmed limes and coconuts here.

More modern history played a direct role in establishing the park's main trail. Back in the 1960s Elliott Key, the primary island in Biscayne National Park, was in the throes of being developed. At the same time environmentalists were fighting to preserve the key, which was an important habitat for rare flora and fauna, unlike the more developed string of keys both north and south of it. Then, on the day before Key Biscayne was declared a national monument, developers bulldozed a four-lane swath through the center of the island. Today the park service keeps open a trail, only one lane wide, as a reminder of that incident. It is known as "Spite Highway." Biscayne was later designated a national park.

Spite Highway traverses a rich tropical menagerie of flora and avian life and leads to overlooks of the Gulf Stream out in the Atlantic and of clear Biscayne Bay. Elliott Key Trail informs walkers and complements Spite Highway, resulting in a little-known and lesser-used walking area in America's most watery national park.

Elliott Key Trail

Begin: Elliott Key Harbor
End: Elliott Key Visitor Center
Distance: 1.1 miles
Trail Difficulty: Easy
Highlights: Ocean views, tropical hardwood hammock, interpretive information
Hazards: None
Trail Connections: Spite Highway North, Spite Highway South
Season: Winter
Maps: Biscayne National Park map
Trailhead: Hikers must take private boat to Elliott Key or commercial ferry from Convoy Point Visitor Center. Once on Elliott Key, look north toward the campground; the trail starts near the swim area.

This is an interpretive trail that winds through the heart of Elliott Key. Along the way it traverses the environments of the island and features displays about the history and nature of the area. Start your walk near Elliott Key Harbor. A sign with a map marks the trail.

Leave the grassy field by the harbor and enter a thick and shady hardwood hammock. There are many tall trees overhead: tamarind, poisonwood, strangler fig, mahogany, and gumbo limbo. A thick understory of dense cover is ideal for wildlife, if not for viewing it. Raccoons are the largest mammals, besides a few rangers, to reside on the island.

At 0.1 mile, skirt the edge of a wet mangrove lowland and turn right. Keep in the tall trees, which are much larger than the younger hammock species of Spite Highway. Watch for a dense patch of leather fern on your left before crossing Spite Highway North at 0.4 mile. The canopy opens somewhat, especially as you near the Atlantic Ocean. After gaining sea views, turn right and begin to follow a boardwalk that skirts the shoreline.

Look out on the Gulf of Mexico; offshore lies the Gulf Stream, the ocean current that runs north off the coast of Florida and heads northeast. European colonizers used the Gulf Stream to return to their homelands from exploring the New World. While the Gulf Stream aided their

Figure 2. Elliott Key offers great views of the Atlantic Ocean. Photo by Johnny Molloy

travel, it also ran perilously close to Elliott Key and the keys to the south, often resulting in shipwrecks in the shallow waters. Today divers explore the underwater outer reaches of Biscayne National Park, checking out these underwater remnants of the past.

Leave the boardwalk at 0.7 mile and come to the grassy oceanside part of the island campground. Grab one last ocean view before reentering the woods. The trail is wider here. Intersect Spite Highway at 0.9 mile. Spite Highway North leaves to the right; Spite Highway South to the left. Pass through the junction on the Elliott Key Trail and come to the wide Breezeway. End your walk at 1.1 mile at the island visitor center overlooking Biscayne Bay.

Spite Highway North

Begin: Elliott Key Trail
End: Atlantic Ocean near Sands Cut
Distance: 2.4 miles
Trail Difficulty: Moderate
Highlights: Tropical hardwood hammock, ocean view, solitude
Hazards: Insects
Trail Connections: Elliott Key Trail, Spite Highway South
Season: Winter
Maps: Biscayne National Park map
Trailhead: Hikers must take private boat to Elliott Key or commercial ferry from Convoy Point Visitor Center. Once on Elliott Key, take Elliott Key Trail east up the Breezeway to Spite Highway. Turn left to take Spite Highway North.

This trail follows the path of what might have been a highway roaring down through the keys. Conservationists banded together to stop the highway from being built and succeeded in getting the island set aside as Biscayne National Monument, now Biscayne National Park. However, in 1968, on the day before the land was to be turned over, developers cut a four-lane-wide swath through the center of Elliott Key, a spiteful act of anger over not getting the highway authorized. This swath grew back, but park personnel have kept one "lane" of Spite Highway open for visitors to walk through a nicely recovering hammock and to remind visitors of what might have been.

Spite Highway North leads from near Elliott Key Harbor to the Atlantic Ocean near where an old private home once stood; it was destroyed for good by Hurricane Andrew in 1992. Chances are you will be the only one hiking this trail.

From the visitor center, walk east on the Elliott Key Trail up the wide grassy Breezeway for 0.2 mile to reach Spite Highway. The trail leaving on the right is Spite Highway South. To your left is Spite Highway North. Turn left here and enter the recovering hardwood hammock. Trees such as Jamaica dogwood, gumbo limbo, poisonwood, strangler fig, and tall tamarinds are regaining their former stature in the center of Elliott Key.

The thick understory and the dense canopy form a shady tunnel through which to hike. Below you is crumbled limestone. Watch out for spider webs—the multilegged creatures love to catch other bugs traveling Spite Highway. Also, watch the dragonflies as they hunt from the air for insects. These two sets of predators are working to keep down the mosquito population, which can be high much of the time.

At 0.2 mile, bisect the Elliott Key Trail. Keep forward, heading north down a path that jogs left and right, rarely keeping a perfectly straight path. At mile 1.4, come to a lower, wetter parcel of land and observe the buttonwoods that thrive here. It is not high or dry enough for the surrounding hammock trees.

Look around for small palms; a few of these are Sargent's cherry palms, which grow in the wild almost exclusively on Elliott Key. The species generally resembles a royal palm but is much smaller. In the past, attempts have been made to reintroduce the cherry palm to Long Key and Sands Key, but Elliott Key remains its stronghold. You may also see ocean debris, such as crab trap buoys, on the woodland floor. These have been deposited onto the center of the island during powerful hurricanes. Imagine what it would be like on this island during a big blow.

At mile 2.0 Spite Highway begins to veer right, to the east. Finally, you leave the thick tropical hammock and pass through some sea grapes and nickerbean, which has nasty curled thorns that will positively grasp you. There is a nice little grassy area with a few coconut palms near the water. At mile 2.4, emerge onto a small beach and the Atlantic Ocean. The tower at Fowley Rocks is visible off to your left. Sands Cut and Sands Key are out of sight to the north. Bache Shoal and Triumph Reef are to the east. Just think: had the highway been built, this might be the site of a convenience store.

Spite Highway South

Begin: Elliott Key Trail
End: South end of Elliott Key
Distance: 4.0 miles
Trail Difficulty: Easy
Highlights: Ocean view, tropical hardwood hammock, rare butterfly habitat
Hazards: Insects
Trail Connections: Spite Highway North, Elliott Key Trail
Season: Winter
Maps: Biscayne National Park map
Trailhead: Hikers must take private boat to Elliott Key or commercial ferry from Convoy Point Visitor Center. Once on Elliott Key, take Elliott Key Trail 0.2 mile east up the Breezeway to Spite Highway. Turn right to take Spite Highway South.

This trail traces Spite Highway to the south end of Elliott Key, following the swath cut by developers before the island was taken over by the National Park Service (see Spite Highway North for a little more history). This path has more directional and vegetational variation than Spite Highway North, passing through buttonwood groves and tropical hardwood hammocks before dead-ending near Adams Key. Two side trails allow good views of both the Atlantic Ocean at Petrel Point and Biscayne Bay in Sandwich Cove.

Spite Highway South is also known for its butterflies. Its most renowned resident is Schaus' swallowtail butterfly. The insect's primary dwelling place is Elliott Key, where the larvae thrive in the torchwood and wild lime trees in the tropical hammocks. Each year, from April through June, butterfly enthusiasts walk this path, looking for the rare beauties as they flutter through the hammocks.

Start your hike on Spite Highway South in a low buttonwood forest. At 0.2 mile—after leaving the junction with Elliott Key Trail—you come to an actual hill that rises two feet! This rise is enough to support the tropical hardwood hammock for which Elliott Key is known, and the hill is the most radical vertical variation on the entire island trail system.

At 0.6 mile, drop just a few inches and the forest changes back to low buttonwood forest, which continues off and on. Where there are hardwood hammocks look for vegetated mounds or piles of soil on either side of the path. These may be left over from hurricanes or from the clearing of Spite Highway.

At mile 2.1, veer left and enter a long stretch of open buttonwood lands. The ground is lower here. The understory is grass and/or sea purslane. At times it resembles the coastal prairie of the Everglades near Flamingo. The low open stretch of buttonwood continues for a half mile before hardwood hammock resumes.

At mile 2.9, come to a trail junction. A wide side trail leads left 0.3 mile through a shady tunnel to Petrel Point, where there is a limestone shore backed by buttonwood and sea grape. Concrete foundations of a house and piled wood indicate former habitation. This may have been a farm dwelling. Back in the early 1900s limes and pineapples were cultivated here. A hurricane in 1925 washed most of the topsoil away, ending the farming on Elliott Key. The Atlantic Ocean and Hawk Channel lie to your east. Also at mile 2.9 there is also a narrow side trail to the right, which may or may not be maintained, following a grown-over road through a hardwood hammock then through buttonwood to end at Sandwich Cove, where the pilings of a dock are out in the water.

Keep south on Spite Highway. Notice the numerous tall tamarind and Jamaica dogwood trees toward the south end of Elliott Key. The path is rocky at your feet. At mile 4.0 the trail ends in a turnaround bordered by buttonwood. Spite Highway once continued beyond here, but it is indistinct and grown over and not recommended for travel.

Hiking Trails of Everglades National Park

Mention the Everglades and water comes to mind. After all, it is known as the "River of Grass." The Everglades are actually a mosaic of numerous ecosystems, from sawgrass plains to pinelands, tropical hardwood hammocks, and coastal prairies to sandy islands in the Gulf of Mexico. Among these ecosystems are many hiking trails for which the Everglades is undeservedly lesser known.

For hikers, paths range from short nature trails to miles-long paths with overnight camping possibilities. If you decide to trek overnight, you must get a permit from one of the ranger stations for backcountry camping. When considering camping, keep in mind that in recent years the Everglades have seen the rise of an unsettling new exotic visitor: pythons. They grow up to nine feet long in their first year, unsettling pet owners enough to drop them off in the Everglades. And these pythons feel right at home—they breed in the wild. Rangers have found females full of eggs and have killed pythons as large as fifteen feet long.

The most extensive trail network is in the pinelands, specifically Long Pine Key. Gated fire roads head in every direction in this most diverse of ecosystems, the home of the endangered Florida panther. Rich tropical hammocks dot the pinelands, which are underlain with limestone. This limestone, eroded into unusual shapes and patterns, often shows itself under the slash pines.

Birds can be observed nearly everywhere your feet can take you. And yes, there are alligators, especially in the canals alongside trails. Old Ingraham Highway, a road turned trail, offers a trip into the heart of the Everglades, where the soundscape is nothing but natural.

Things get a bit saltier down Flamingo way. Trails trace raised roadbeds alongside brackish canals, beneath lush tropical woodlands that thrive in the south of Florida. From Flamingo the Coastal Prairie Trail heads west through a buttonwood forest and along open marl swaths to a beach along Florida Bay. The Snake Bight Trail ends at an observation platform at Florida Bay.

A separate access route to the park, Shark Valley, is immersed in the "river of grass" off the Tamiami Trail. It offers a paved loop trail and two fascinating nature trails, the Bobcat Boardwalk and the Otter Cave Trail.

Out on the Gulf side of the park, entered through Everglades City, there is even a trail that can only be reached by boat—Sandfly Island Nature Trail. This path is on one of the Ten Thousand Islands. Hikers must first paddle or powerboat themselves to this key, which is an old shell mound first occupied by Calusa Indians and later by white settlers. Now you can take a walk on the island and see the remains of when families called this "back of beyond" home.

Trail Updates at a Glance

· Coastal Prairie Trail is closed due to extensive hurricane damage
· Eco Pond is closed due to extensive hurricane damage
· Guy Bradley Trail is temporarily closed due to hurricane damage

Anhinga Trail

Begin: Royal Palm Hammock Visitor Center
End: Royal Palm Hammock Visitor Center
Distance: 0.8-mile loop
Trail Difficulty: Wheelchair accessible
Highlights: Wildlife
Hazards: Alligators, mosquitoes
Trail Connections: Gumbo Limbo Trail
Season: Year-round
Maps: Everglades National Park map
Trailhead: From the Ernest Coe Visitor Center, follow Main Park Road for 1.6 miles to the turnoff to Royal Palm Hammock. Turn left and follow this road for 1.9 miles to where it ends in the parking area.

For most visitors, the Anhinga Trail is their first and perhaps only glimpse into Everglades National Park. Its proximity to the park entrance guarantees its popularity, and wildlife here is so common and complacent that you may hear people asking, "Is that alligator real?" Rest assured they are.

From the visitor center follow the broad paved path—a segment of the original Homestead-to-Flamingo Ingraham Highway—along Taylor Slough, one of the few waterways in this portion of the park that retains water year-round, no matter how bad the drought may be elsewhere. The water makes this a haven for wildlife. Cormorants hang out along the stone wall; alligators sun on the grass. Walk down to the end of the pavement, passing a boardwalk on the left at 0.2 mile, and walk straight ahead to an observation deck with a view over the marsh. In spring you'll see nesting egrets, herons, and roseate spoonbills in the trees.

Return and turn right to follow the boardwalk along the slough. Alligators hang out on the hummocky islands. The odd-looking cluster of trees is made up of pond apple, a South Florida native tree with thick trunks and a fruit that appeals to raccoons and other wildlife but not to humans—it tastes like turpentine. Cormorants favor the pond apple trees and the roof of the rain shelter.

Continue along the boardwalk to a spur trail on the right. Follow this out to an observation platform over a broader part of the slough, where alligators drift through the inky water. Return to the main path and turn right. The boardwalk offers expansive views of the sawgrass prairies off to the right before it ends again at the paved trail. Turn right and take your time, enjoying the wildlife as you return to the parking area.

Bayshore Loop

Begin: Coastal Prairie Trail
End: Coastal Prairie Trail
Distance: 1.3-mile loop
Trail Difficulty: Moderate
Highlights: Views of Florida Bay and coastal prairie, birding
Hazards: Mosquitoes, sun, mud
Trail Connections: Coastal Prairie Trail
Season: Winter–spring
Maps: Everglades National Park map
Trailhead: From the Flamingo Visitor Center, drive west on Main Park Road for 1 mile to the Flamingo Campground. Proceed past the check-in station to C Loop. The Coastal Prairie Trail begins at a trailhead in the very back of the C loop and is used to access the Bayshore Loop.

Providing a short loop walk through the mangrove-lined edge of Florida Bay and the unique coastal prairie habitat, the Bayshore Loop is an excellent sampler of what some of the Flamingo area's longer trails (Coastal Prairie, Christian Point) have to offer. Along the waterfront it passes through what was once the original fishing village of Flamingo, with a relic that still recalls this almost-forgotten outpost at the end of the Florida Peninsula. And a plus for hikers who want to dawdle and do some birdwatching along the shore is that unlike on most of the Flamingo area hikes, no bicycles are allowed on this trail.

Start your hike at the Coastal Prairie Trail trailhead on an old cotton pickers' road headed west. Brackish pools reflect the remains of what is left of the not-so-salt-tolerant buttonwoods after the last storm surge thoroughly salted their roots. After 0.2 mile, the Bayshore Loop begins at a sign on your left. Turn left. Pink and white hibiscus bloom along the edge of the salt hay footpath. Ducking under black mangroves, you catch the seaside aroma of Florida Bay before you see it, a ribbon of silver beyond the clusters of mangroves. Seagrass streamers flutter in the low branches, and the wrack line is strewn with horseshoe crabs, bumpers, buoys, and other flotsam of the craft that ply Florida Bay.

Turn right and follow the footpath behind the mangroves, just out of the way of the waves. At 0.4 mile, the trail emerges at a broad opening, a beach between the mangroves, with a hardpacked mat of seagrass atop the mucky marl that otherwise makes up the bottom and edges of the bay. You pass a distinctive multitrunked palm tree at 0.5 mile, and the trail turns abruptly to the right. Keep alert for a cistern in the woods to your right, a remnant of the old fishing village. The trail curves around buttonwoods and leads you through clusters of saltwort. After 0.7 mile, the Bayshore Loop begins its loop back toward the Coastal Prairie Trail, leaving the water's edge for good as it veers to the right; one last side spur leads out to an overlook on Florida Bay, where the birding is superb.

Keep right at the next junction, where the view opens up to showcase the coastal prairie. A few moments later, you reach the Coastal Prairie Trail at 0.8 mile. Turn right and check your balance, as the merest drop of rain on the marl surface of the footpath will make it feel as if you're walking across an oil slick. Clusters of yaupon holly show off their red berries. After 1.1 miles, the trail leaves the coastal prairie and enters the buttonwood stand, where you reach the beginning of the Bayshore Loop. Continue straight down the road to the trailhead to finish your 1.3-mile hike.

Bear Lake Trail

Begin: Bear Lake trailhead
End: Bear Lake
Distance: 1.8 miles one way
Trail Difficulty: Easy
Highlights: Great birding at Bear Lake and along the Homestead Canal
Hazards: Mosquitoes
Trail Connections: None
Season: Winter
Maps: Everglades National Park map
Trailhead: From the Flamingo Visitor Center, follow Main Park Road north for 0.5 mile to Bear Lake Road. Turn left to follow Bear Lake Road, an unpaved road that is frequently closed after heavy rains, for 1.7 miles as it parallels the Buttonwood Canal. The road ends at the trailhead parking area with a canoe symbol sign.

Paralleling the former Homestead Canal, an attempt by early developers to drain the coastal prairies around Cape Sable, the Bear Lake Trail takes you on a journey down an old road built of limestone fill scooped from the canal diggings. Starting at the trailhead, the trail leads you down a corridor surrounded by tropical forest, with the mangrove-lined canal (now called the Bear Lake Canal, and popular with canoeists) as your constant companion. At the end of the hike lies Bear Lake, a brackish body of water that makes for a scenic destination.

The Bear Lake Trail begins just beyond the "No Parking Beyond This Sign" sign. Once a dark corridor under a dense canopy of tropical trees, it has had its shade peeled away by the rapacious winds of Hurricanes Katrina and Wilma. Though battered, gumbo-limbo trees still stand as guardians along the path. Canoeists must portage the first 0.1 mile to a put in at a small dock. Round the gate to continue down the trail, where bicycles are permitted.

In 1922 eager developers attempted to connect Homestead and Cape Sable via this unfinished highway. In their draining and digging of ditches, they severely changed the surrounding ecosystem. Where once this area was a dense tropical forest as you see on the left, the intrusion of salt water from Florida Bay into the canal system encouraged mangroves to flourish, as you see on the right. Between the two habitats, the canal water shimmers the color of latte.

Look up and around you. Cardinal wild pine, a showy bromeliad, dangles overhead from trees arching over the trail. Spindly semaphore cactus climbs up tree trunks. A tiny thrinax palm, more commonly found in the Keys, grows along the edge of the trail. By 0.6 mile, the mangrove forest crowds in on both sides. On the far side of the canal, you begin to see coastal prairie with clumps of buttonwood.

Rocks and roots protrude from the footpath before it drops down and veers to the left near a spoil bank created by the digging of the canal. After a mile the canal broadens, its surface alive with water bugs. Veering right to parallel the canal again, the trail becomes a narrow track crowded by vegetation, edging ever closer to the water. The canal broadens, splitting into multiple channels through a dangling curtain of mangrove roots.

Keep going west, and Bear Lake becomes visible through the trees to your left at 1.6 miles. You cross a 'gator slide, and the trail comes to an end on the shores of Bear Lake, where the Calusa once camped and harvested the marine riches of the lake, leaving behind a shell mound in the vicinity. If the mosquitoes permit, pull up a log and enjoy the view from the little marl beach, watching herons and egrets perch in the mangroves and alligators drift slowly across the tannic waters.

As you turn around to retrace your steps back along this linear trail, keep alert on the right for a lignum vitae tree on the right. Found primarily in the Keys and Caribbean, it is the "tree of life," with dense wood, purported healing properties, and an unusual and distinct growth habit—its limbs cross back over each other as they grow.

Bobcat Boardwalk

Begin: Shark Valley Visitor Center
End: Shark Valley Visitor Center
Distance: 0.3-mile loop
Trail Difficulty: Wheelchair accessible
Highlights: Immersion into tropical hammocks
Hazards: Mosquitoes
Trail Connections: Otter Cave Trail
Season: Fall–spring
Maps: Everglades National Park map
Trailhead: From the intersection of Krome Avenue (SR 997) and the Tamiami Trail (US 41) at the entrance to the Miccosukee reservation, drive 18 miles west. The entrance is on the left. The park is open from 8:30 a.m. to 6:00 p.m. There is a $10 per car entrance fee; your receipt is good for entrance at any other unit of Everglades National Park for one week.

Shark Valley is a popular destination in winter and spring to see migratory and nesting birds. Most visitors opt to bike or take the tram around the 14-mile paved loop through the River of Grass, which provides a stop at a tall observation tower along the route. For folks who walk a portion of the paved loop, the Bobcat Boardwalk is always a part of their explorations. Although the boardwalk used to be mostly a shady tunnel, the tree canopy was ripped off by Hurricane Wilma in 2005 and will take a few years to return.

Walk behind the visitor center and follow the paved trail paralleling the canal. In a few moments you come to the Bobcat Boardwalk trailhead on the left. Turn left and follow the boardwalk into a bayhead swamp. It continues across an open sawgrass prairie with nice views. Purple pickerelweed blooms rise out of water-filled solution holes in the prairie. The boardwalk meanders into a stand of willows. A bench lets you rest above a flowing stream. Entering the tropical hardwood hammock, you can see that the trees have been battered but are still recognizable—cocoplum with its round leaves, white stopper with its skunky smell. Under a canopy, a set of benches provides a shady stop.

The boardwalk makes a sharp left and crosses more open prairie onto another tropical hammock island thick with fallen trees.

You emerge at the paved loop at an interpretive sign explaining periphyton, the goopy-looking greenish brown blobs that float everywhere and are the primary biomass of the Everglades. Exit from the boardwalk and turn left to follow the paved loop back around to the visitor center.

Christian Point Trail

Begin: Main Park Road
End: Christian Point
Distance: 2.1 miles one way
Trail Difficulty: Strenuous
Highlights: Numerous air plants, views of Florida Bay, birding
Hazards: Mosquitoes, sun, mud
Trail Connections: None
Season: Winter
Maps: Everglades National Park map
Trailhead: From the Flamingo Visitor Center, follow Main Park Road north for 0.8 mile to the Christian Point trailhead on the right.

This is one of the more challenging trails in Flamingo, especially after the storm surge damage of Hurricanes Katrina and Wilma. After traversing a mangrove forest and entering a small prairie, Christian Point Trail winds around in a hammock of buttonwood covered with epiphytes and then opens onto a large marl prairie, where the trail can be muddy. On the far side of this prairie—just north of Christian Point, beyond a wooded shoreline—lies Snake Bight, part of Florida Bay. This is a potentially good birding site, overlooking open shallows.

Start your hike by entering the mangrove forest and crossing a wet area on a boardwalk. Mangroves are all around you. The trunk of the red mangrove lies atop numerous prop roots, which act as buttresses and allow the tree to take oxygen directly from the air. At 0.1 mile, emerge from the forest onto a small marl prairie. The Flamingo microwave tower is visible from here. Work south to enter a buttonwood forest at 0.3 mile. The trail winds around and below the remains of large buttonwoods that did not survive the intrusion of salt from the hurricanes' storm surges. Notice the epiphytes, or air plants, that grow on the horizontal branches. Wild pineapple is the prevalent epiphyte here. These air plants grow in the crooks of trees and wherever else they can gain purchase. Nutrient-absorbing organs in epiphytes allow them to get nutrients from rainfall.

At 0.6 mile, intersect an old road and begin to turn east just past a trail sign. The path remains very curvy, even though it follows the old roadbed. Look for tropical trees such as poisonwood, Jamaica dogwood, and strangler fig and other hammock plants, such as soapberry and white stopper.

There is another marl prairie at mile 1.3; this one is very large. Look back for another view of the tower at Flamingo. At mile 1.7, enter an open marl prairie with shoe-sucking mud. Persistent hikers continue east, staying with a trail that sometimes winds through saltwort and sometimes across open marl. After 2 miles, you enter a forest of buttonwood and black mangrove. Come to the edge of the continent at mile 2.1, where there are views of Snake Bight and the rest of Florida Bay. The shoreline trees act as an effective blind for viewing bird life, which can be abundant here.

Coastal Prairie Trail

Begin: Flamingo Campground
End: Clubhouse Beach
Distance: 5.6 miles one way
Trail Difficulty: Very difficult
Highlights: Marl prairie, Clubhouse Beach, Florida Bay vistas, backcountry camping
Hazards: Extreme mud, insects, sun
Trail Connections: Bayshore Loop
Season: Winter
Maps: Everglades National Park map
Trailhead: From the Flamingo Visitor Center, drive west on Main Park Road for one mile to Flamingo Campground. Proceed past the check-in station to C Loop. The Coastal Prairie Trail begins in the very back of the C loop.

This is the most southerly trail on the U.S. mainland. It actually heads west, paralleling the coast of Florida Bay toward Cape Sable, in a mixture of buttonwood forest and open marl prairie, to end at Clubhouse Beach on Florida Bay. Clubhouse Beach is a designated backcountry campsite.

Unfortunately, the hurricanes of 2005 obliterated the Coastal Prairie Trail, and it is closed as of this writing. Everglades National Park has many other hurricane-related restoration priorities; reopening of this trail is intended but may take a while.

East Long Pine Key Loop

Begin: Long Pine Key Campground
End: Long Pine Key Campground
Distance: 4.5-mile loop
Trail Difficulty: Moderate
Highlights: Pine rocklands, tropical hardwood hammock, solitude
Hazards: Mud, sharp rocks
Trail Connections: Long Pine Key Nature Trail
Season: Winter
Maps: Long Pine Key trails handout from visitor center
Trailhead: From the Ernest Coe Visitor Center, drive west on Main Park Road for 6 miles to Long Pine Key Road. Turn left and follow Long Pine Key Road for 1 mile to Gate G3, which is on your left just before the turn into the campground.

This hike explores the lesser-visited east side of Long Pine Key, using old jeep roads to explore the pine rocklands that have become so rare in South Florida. The hike leads you east from the campground area, immediately passing a species-rich hardwood hammock before you cross open sawgrass prairies to intersect Research Road. Walk a bit on Research Road and head back north by an Everglades pond before passing through Long Pine Key Campground to complete your loop.

To begin your hike, start walking east and pass around Gate G3. Immediately to your left is a tropical hardwood hammock where tamarind, gumbo-limbo, and cocoplum flourish. On your right are classic pine rocklands: tall, well-spaced Dade County slash pines with an understory of grass and saw palmettos and a base of jagged karst—limestone with solution holes and other surface features created by erosion.

This pine forest is fire dependent. Before Everglades National Park was created, lightning started fires. After the park was created, fires were suppressed. Today park staff perform prescribed burns to maintain the pine rocklands habitat, which would vanish if the understory hardwoods, especially the oaks, had a chance to take over. The jeep roads through this area serve as firebreaks for the prescribed burns, so you'll often see completely different habitats on opposite sides of the road.

The pine rocklands give way to an open sawgrass prairie at 0.3 mile. Here the land is slightly lower and is inundated longer during the wet season, effectively barring pine growth on the karst. At 0.6 mile, you reenter the pine forest before turning sharply south. At 0.8 mile, there is a trail junction. Veer left and continue east through open pine forest to traverse another sawgrass glade with extensive views to the south.

You reach the next trail junction at mile 1.6. To your left is a dead-end trail. If you wish to follow this spur, it leads 0.3 mile to the edge of a hardwood hammock before veering east, then north. The jeep trail becomes increasingly muddy as it skirts the edge of a glade before entering bona fide wetlands where water flows most of the year. The river of grass bars this side trail after 1.2 miles, where you can see cars on the Main Park Road but cannot access it without major slogging through the sawgrass prairie—not recommended unless you're prepared for the razor edges of the grass and the rock underfoot.

From the aforementioned trail junction, the East Long Pine Key Loop turns right, heading south through more open pine rocklands where there are many standing dead snags. After 2 miles, the trail veers to the southwest. Step around Gate G2 just before you reach Research Road at 2.4 miles. Turn right and follow the east-west corridor of Research Road. This paved road cuts a narrow swath through the pinelands. Look for a low wet area on your right before coming to Gate G2A at mile 2.8. At this point, another side trail leads north and provides a shortcut back to the beginning of this hike. Should you choose to explore it, this side trail traverses especially rocky pineland, where the karst bedrock, with its many sharp edges and small holes, is very evident. Pass a small hammock on your left at 0.4 mile before coming to a trail junction at 0.9 mile. You were at this intersection back at mile 0.8 of the East Long Pine Key Loop Hike and can backtrack from there.

If you are following the main route, keep walking along Research Road. A canal parallels the road, and it is lined with poisonwood, cocoplum, and Brazilian pepper. Look for fish in the canal. At mile 3.5 you reach Gate G2B on your right. Bridge the small canal here as you turn right and head north. You'll soon come to a pond on your right with a bench for taking a break. Beyond this pond, pine prevails, but it is very dispersed.

Come to the south end of Long Pine Key Campground at mile 4.0. Stay left and walk through the campground, passing a lake on your left. Leave the campground road and turn right, coming to Gate G3 to complete your loop at 4.5 miles.

Gumbo Limbo Trail

Begin: Royal Palm Hammock Visitor Center
End: Royal Palm Hammock Visitor Center
Distance: 0.4-mile loop
Trail Difficulty: Wheelchair accessible
Highlights: Large solution holes
Hazards: Poison ivy, mosquitoes
Trail Connections: Anhinga Trail
Season: Year-round
Maps: Everglades National Park map
Trailhead: From the Ernest Coe Visitor Center, follow Main Park Road for 1.6 miles to the turnoff to Royal Palm Hammock. Turn left and follow this road for 1.9 miles to where it ends in the parking area.

At Royal Palm Hammock, the Gumbo Limbo Trail is a paved path that gets you up close and personal with a tropical hammock on what was once called Paradise Key, when this area was a state park. Although it's a short walk, it has some interesting highlights. It used to be a lushly canopied walk entirely in shade, but Hurricane Wilma stripped off the tree canopy, mainly leaves and smaller branches. Within a few years, the deep shade should return.

The trail starts at the "Gumbo Limbo Trail" sign next to a royal palm just outside the visitor center. Peeling gumbo-limbo trees show off their odd green and red bark, leaning heavily across the trail and clipped off in places. Look closely and you'll see young royal palms rising from the crowded understory. In several lush spots, poison ivy is prevalent along the edges of the footpath. So is wild coffee, which has crinkly-looking leaves and bright reddish brown berries. Interpretive signs point out some of the tropical trees, such as pigeon plum. The air is thick and humid, and sword fern grows well in the understory.

An overlook lets you peer into a solution hole, where bright water spangles float on the dark water. These holes form by the gradual erosion of the limestone bedrock by acidic water as rain flows through the leaves on the forest floor. There are several such holes at different points along the trail. Notice the tree with rounded frond leaves—a paradise tree.

There are also Jamaican satinleaf trees and the poisonwood, a tree with sap ten times more harmful than poison ivy. It is native to the Everglades and best avoided if you have trouble with poison ivy. The nasty-looking oozy dark blotches on the smooth tree trunk are the best way of identifying this tree.

The trail crosses a short boardwalk over a broad solution hole that holds a small marsh. Cattails grow along the edge. As the trail ends, you emerge from the woods facing the visitor center, adjacent to the parking area.

Guy Bradley Trail

Begin: Flamingo Visitor Center
End: Christian Point
Distance: 1.0 mile one way
Trail Difficulty: Easy
Highlights: VIews of Florida Bay
Hazards: Mosquitoes
Trail Connections: None
Season: Winter–spring
Maps: Everglades National Park map
Trailhead: The trail starts at the Guy Bradley Memorial at the Flamingo Visitor Center and follows the waterfront to the campground.

NOTE: This trail was closed in early 2006 due to a severe washout during the Hurricane Wilma storm surge that swamped Flamingo and due to reconstruction of buildings damaged or destroyed along the route. Expect it to reopen in the future.

This short, paved walk is not a venture into nature, but it does offer excellent views of Florida Bay and insight into the evolution of the Everglades National Park. In the early 1900s, naturalists were well aware of the rich bird life in the Everglades, and so were plume hunters, looking to cash in on the use of heron, egret, and spoonbill plumage as a New York fashion statement, a popular finishing touch to ladies' hats. State law provided one game warden for each county in Florida. This was a start, but the wardens had no backup. The Audubon Society stepped up and hired four wardens at its own expense to protect certain rookeries in the state. One of them was Guy Bradley. He was a Monroe County deputy and knew the local hunting community—both legal and poachers—very well.

At the age of thirty-five, the fearless lawman had his last run-in with the plume poachers. On July 8, 1906, Guy Bradley's body was found adrift in his skiff near a prime heron nesting area off Cape Sable. He had died the day before from gunshot wounds. Soon after, Walter Smith admitted to the murder and was arrested and incarcerated in Key West. Smith had threatened to kill Bradley if the warden ever attempted to arrest him or his family and made good on his threat after his son Tom was arrested for poaching. The jury ruled that Smith had acted in self-defense, but the national outrage over the murder and subsequent trial galvanized public opinion, and laws were enacted to protect the nesting bird colonies, one of the Everglades' most precious treasures. The fad of wearing hats decorated by bird feathers soon fell out of vogue, and poaching decreased. But Bradley's martyrdom and the shooting of another warden in 1908 near Charlotte Harbor began the movement that eventually led to the creation of Everglades National Park.

Start your walk by reading the bronze memorial to Guy Bradley, and then head west down the sidewalk toward the Flamingo Lodge. At 0.1 mile, you will come upon a sign with a picture of an amphitheater as well as a no-jeeps-allowed sign. Turn left onto a paved path that soon splits left again and circles behind the lodge and along Florida Bay. Fantastic views of the keys in Florida Bay are interspersed among the stands of black mangrove.

Leaving the lodge behind, you enter a wooded area. Look for pilings of an old dock near the shoreline. The trail is still so close to the ocean that seagrass washes over the path. The seagrass is then cleared and piled along either side of the path. At 0.9 mile a side trail leads to the former rental cottage area. Ahead is the grassy area of the Flamingo walk-in tent campground. The trail ends at the campground parking turnaround, at 1.0 mile.

Long Pine Key Walking Trail and Nature Trail

Begin: Long Pine Key Campground
End: Main Park Road
Distance: 6.4 miles one way
Trail Difficulty: Moderate
Highlights: Hardwood hammocks, Pine Glades Lake
Hazards: Excessive sun
Trail Connections: East Long Pine Key Loop hike
Season: Winter
Maps: Everglades National Park map, Long Pine Key trails handout
Trailhead: From the park entrance, drive east 6 miles to Long Pine Key Road. Turn left on Long Pine Key Road and follow it for 1.4 miles to the picnic area by Long Pine Key Lake.

This hike starts along the shores of Long Pine Key Lake, then darts into a hardwood hammock. It emerges onto the pine rocklands and heads northwest by other hammocks and pine woods. It ends up along the shores of Pine Glades Lake, where you may see an alligator. Backtrack or use other pinelands trails and Main Park Road to make a loop.

Long Pine Key is the most westerly extension of the Miami Rock Ridge. The Miami Rock Ridge is a band of limestone that extends from Miami southwest to Homestead and farther west to end at Long Pine Key. This length of exposed limestone formerly held much biodiversity. Now most of the area has been developed, which makes Long Pine Key, within Everglades National Park, all the more important botanically.

Walk to the very back of the picnic area auto turnaround and begin hiking south along Long Pine Key Lake, which will be on your left. After a short distance look for a trail turning sharply right, away from the lake. This is the Long Pine Key Walking Trail. Soon enter a thick hardwood hammock. This cool and dark place is rich in plant species. All the vegetation helps retain moisture, unlike the pinelands around you.

At 0.2 mile come to a trail junction, turn left and head west, crossing a sawgrass prairie with good views. Come to another junction at 0.3 mile. Turn left, now on the Long Pine Key Nature Trail, and begin to follow the old jeep road on a westerly track. (To the right, the Long Pine Key Nature Trail leads 0.5 mile to Long Pine Key Road near the Long Pine Key campground kiosk.)

Enter a pine woodland, which varies in density. Look at the erosion pattern of the limestone on the left of the trail. It has many pointed sharp edges and is known as "dogtooth" limestone. Pass another tawny prairie before coming to a trail junction at mile 1.2. The nature trail stays left. To the right is a 1-mile side trail that dead-ends in a sawgrass prairie and does not connect to Main Park Road, as shown on some maps.

Continue west in a slash pine woodland, passing a large hardwood hammock on your right. The slash pines here, and in most of South Florida, are considered a distinct subspecies of slash pine, often called Dade County Pine. South Florida slash pine is more fire tolerant and drought resistant than typical slash pines. Pass a second sawgrass prairie at mile 1.9, then enter a dense stand of slash pine. Come to a trail junction at mile 2.3. A side trail leads left 1.2 miles to Research Road.

Stay right and begin to hike north in pine woods with a fairly thick understory. A prominent understory plant is the cocoplum. It grows in moist situations and can be identified by its alternate, dark green, shiny oval leaves. This fruit-bearing plant was a diet staple for all Indians that roamed the 'Glades. The fruits are usually purple, the size of a child's thumb. They are sweet and juicy and have one large seed inside.

At mile 4.0, come to another trail junction. The Long Pine Key Walking and Nature Trail leads left. (To your right is a side trail leading 0.8 mile to Gate 10 on Main Park Road. This side trail starts north, then east, passing many hardwood hammocks along the way.) The Long Pine Key Walking and Nature Trail turns westward through slash pine woods. Pass a sizable hammock on your right at mile 4.7. Intersect another trail at mile 5.3. Stay forward on the nature trail. The trail to your left leads 1.3 miles toward Research Road. All these junctions make the path seem confusing, but following the Long Pine Key Walking and Nature Trail is easy.

Begin to turn north as the pine woods open up, availing good views west. Pass a stand of willow trees on your right before coming to Gate 8 and Pine Glades Lake at mile 5.9. Walk around the lake and look for alligators. This is an artificial lake, created when underlying limestone was extracted from here as fill for Main Park Road. There-and-back day hikers should turn around here, as the last half-mile of the nature trail follows a crumbling paved road to intersect Main Park Road at mile 6.4.

Mahogany Hammock Trail

Begin: Main Park Road
End: Main Park Road
Distance: 0.4-mile loop
Trail Difficulty: Wheelchair accessible
Highlights: Paurotis palm stands and ancient mahogany trees
Hazards: Poison ivy vines dangling from trees
Trail Connections: None
Season: Winter–spring
Maps: Everglades National Park map
Trailhead: From the Ernest Coe Visitor Center, follow Main Park Road for 21 miles toward Flamingo. Turn right at the sign for Mahogany Hammock and follow the road for 1.7 miles to the parking area at the trailhead.

Newly renovated with an updated boardwalk and new interpretive signs, the Mahogany Hammock Trail remains one of my favorites in Everglades National Park for exploring its unique tropical flora. The trail is entirely a boardwalk. It starts by crossing a natural moat of sawgrass prairie to this tree island in the Shark Valley Slough. A showy stand of paurotis palms towers over the entrance to the island. The loop starts here. Continue walking straight ahead. You can see the effects of recent hurricanes everywhere—trees are down all over the island, blanketed by massive poison ivy vines. Although most of the ancient mahogany trees lost their crowns, they are still standing strong. The hammock is rebounding—the chaotic undergrowth is nature's way of repairing damage.

You walk beneath cabbage palms and gumbo-limbo, Jamaican satinleaf (with its fuzzy brown leaf undersides), and cat's-claw. Wild pine shows off brilliant crimson blooms, peeping out of the crooks of trees and atop fallen snags. The largest of the mahoganies is at 0.1 mile, trimmed back by the hurricanes but still hosting a hanging garden draped over its boughs. Watch and listen closely for colorful birds: finches and warblers flitting through the tangled undergrowth.

Turn left and pass a bench next to giant leather ferns. A "nursery log" shows off strap ferns on the right. A fallen tree root ball makes a jungle

Figure 3. Phyllis Malinski studies the paurotis palms from the renovated boardwalk. Photo by Sandra Friend

wall next to a marker on hurricanes. Walk down a straightaway with no shade. The trail turns left at another thicket of paurotis palm, then right past a root ball covered in resurrection fern and a dusting of limestone clumps. Across the boardwalk are more paurotis palms—they have become more noticeable and showy with the tropical canopy missing.

Poison ivy suffocates a cabbage palm across from the next bench. The boardwalk turns left past more palms and meanders through the verdant wreckage of the understory. Crimson coral bean blooms poke up through the tangle of vines. Duck under a tree leaning over the boardwalk. Look closely at the peeling gumbo-limbo bark. The trail makes a sharp left, and you catch a whiff of salt from distant mangrove flats. The next bench is catty-corner from a huge strangler fig. Walk through a cool spot under the mastic just before the loop ends at the first palm stand. Turn right to exit.

Mangrove Trail

Begin: Main Park Road
End: Main Park Road
Distance: 0.4-mile loop
Trail Difficulty: Wheelchair accessible
Highlights: Mangrove tunnel and views of West Lake
Hazards: Mosquitoes
Trail Connections: None
Season: Winter–spring
Maps: Everglades National Park map
Trailhead: From the Flamingo Visitor Center, follow Main Park Road north for 7 miles to the West Lake sign on the right. Turn right and park near the "Mangrove Trail" sign.

Figure 4. The boardwalk at West Lake tunnels through mangrove. Photo by Sandra Friend

Despite the extreme weather Florida endures each summer, its mangrove forests are surprisingly resilient. At West Lake the Mangrove Trail loops through a forest that has seen its share of hurricane-related damage, from salty mud flats deposited by Hurricane Donna to the storm surges of 2005 from Hurricanes Katrina and Wilma. Yet this walk still leads you through a shady tunnel, showcasing the protector of Florida's coastline, the mighty mangrove.

Follow the boardwalk into the shady mangrove forest, where bromeliads of various shapes and sizes cling to the gnarled branches of the mangroves. Giant leather ferns rise from the forest floor. During the dry season spiders spin webs between the thousands of pneumatophores protruding from the sand like tiny fingers. These are the breathing roots of the black mangroves. You reach the beginning of the loop. Turn left to walk out to West Lake. Red mangroves line the edge of the lake, standing tall on their roots. The roots are covered with a layer of thick salt, which the plants transpire as they soak in the brackish water. There are benches where the boardwalk heads out farther to give you great views of this massive lake. The boardwalk returns to the shade of the mangrove forest, completing the loop. Continue straight out to exit.

North Pinelands Trail

Begin: Main Park Road
End: Main Park Road
Distance: 3.8 miles
Trail Difficulty: Difficult for the distance
Highlights: Solution holes, Everglades views, hardwood hammocks, solitude
Hazards: Mud, water, sun
Trail Connections: None
Season: Winter
Maps: Long Pine Key trails handout
Trailhead: From the park entrance, drive 8.4 miles to Gate 9, which will be on your right. The North Pinelands Trail starts here.

This is a challenging trail. It meanders along the border of two ecosystems—pinelands and sawgrass prairie. Leave Main Park Road and enter a wet area where you will be one with the river of grass, slogging through water at times above your boot tops. On both sides of the trail are deep and large solution holes, where the clear water reveals the watery life in these limestone "ponds." There is little shade even when pines and hardwoods become more prevalent.

Start the trail by descending north off Main Park Road at Gate 9 on a muddy jeep trail. The path soon turns right and skirts a sawgrass prairie on your left and open pine woods to your right. The path here can be underwater, anything from a couple of inches to halfway up your shin. In other places there will be mud and periphyton, the organisms that act as a filter in the shallows beneath sawgrass. It also is an important part of the food chain, as it houses larvae of small invertebrates (including mosquitoes and deerflies) upon which larger elements of the food chain feed. And so it goes up the chain. The water, imperceptibly flowing across the road, will be clear. Leave the wettest areas at mile 1.0, where occasional small crossflows cover the path.

There are numerous solution holes all around. These solution holes are formed when the top of the limestone erodes and collapses, leaving a void, which fills with water and becomes a haven for all sorts of Everglades creatures, from minnows to crawdads. As more dry land appears at mile 1.8, so do hammock trees, such as tamarind and poisonwood. Sawgrass, whether in clumps or prairies, is always present. Solution holes add a watery context, and pine trees are never far away. The end result is an interesting hodge-podge of microenvironments all around. This is to be expected where ecosystems blend.

At mile 2.2, the trail turns back to the southeast. There is much less mud. However, an advantage of a muddy trail is seeing the tracks of all the animals that traverse the area. The sawgrass prairie stays off to your left and the sky overhead is a constant in this nearly shadeless land. Even the hardwood hammock at mile 3.1 was burned and is now regenerating. Other thriving hammocks are off in the distance on both sides of the trail.

By the time you can hear the cars of Main Park Road, the trail is quite dry. Pass Gate 11 just before coming to Main Park Road at mile 3.8, the end of the trail. To your right it is 2.2 miles back to the trailhead on Main Park Road, so that a 6.0-mile loop can be made by heading west along that road back to the trailhead.

Old Ingraham Highway Trail

Begin: Long Pine Key
End: Old Ingraham campsite
Distance: 10.5 miles one way
Trail Difficulty: Difficult due to distance
Highlights: Cypress domes, solitude, bird life, backcountry campsites
Hazards: Excessive sun, snakes, deer flies, old pavement
Trail Connections: None
Season: Winter
Maps: Everglades National Park map
Trailhead: From the park entrance, drive east on Main Park Road for 3 miles to Royal Palm Hammock Road. Turn left and follow Royal Palm Hammock Road for 0.8 mile to Research Road. Turn right on Research Road and follow it for 0.5 mile to a gravel road heading forward. (Research Road turns right.) Stay forward on the gravel road and follow it for 0.9 mile to end at Gate 15. The Old Ingraham Highway Trail starts behind Gate 15. When parking do not block this gate.

This trail follows the original road that connected the fishing village of Flamingo at Florida Bay to the town of Homestead. Now the Old Ingraham Highway quietly leads into the heart of the lower Everglades to end in the middle of nowhere—or everywhere, if you love this unique environment. Here the expanse of the park envelops you—tree islands and cypress domes rising amid a seemingly endless river of grass. The only sounds you hear are anhingas and other birds announcing your arrival, an alligator splashing into the trailside canal, and the rustle of wind blowing through the trees.

There are downsides to this trail, though. The path is mostly asphalt in decay—and potentially hard on the feet. The canopy is open overhead more often than not, which can result in a sun whipping. Deer flies can dive-bomb your head and scalp beyond mere annoyance. And the area has gained a reputation for being "snakey." To go there and back makes a long 21-mile day hike, which is partly why there are two backcountry campsites on the trail. Leave early in the morning if day hiking, or hike as far as you please and turn around at any point.

Start your hike by walking around Gate 15 and heading south on the Old Ingraham Highway. This was named after a vice president of the Florida East Coast Railroad, J. E. Ingraham, who was instrumental in persuading his company to donate land in 1916 to the Florida Federation of Women's Clubs, where Royal Palm Hammock now stands. Royal Palm Hammock was first known as Paradise Key and was first a Florida state park. On Old Ingraham Highway there is a canal off to your right the entire way. This was dug to obtain fill to raise the road above the waterline. The water here is crystal clear and full of fish. Trees such as poisonwood, willow, and cocoplum line the path. There are enough clear areas to gain many views of the sawgrass prairie.

Pass a side road leading right at 0.6 mile. Look on your left at mile 1.6 for a water monitoring station off in the 'Glades. An old water gauge is a half mile farther. These gauges keep governmental officials apprised of water levels in various parts of the Everglades. There are also intermittent survey markers on the left side of the road. At mile 3.1, bisect two cypress domes, where the woods are high and the trail is shady.

The trail begins to curve to the right, to the east. Another measuring station is on dry land at mile 3.5. You are now heading due east, coming to the Ernest Coe backcountry campsite on your right at mile 3.7. This site is a grass flat that has dry ground suitable for a few tents. No ground fires are allowed here or at the Old Ingraham campsite. Just south of the camp is an area once known as Madiera Farms. Here several miles of canals were dug in the 1930s to drain the land for farming. But the Depression was on. and the farming operation went broke before the first crop was raised. However, the canals attracted a lot of wildlife, especially during the dry season, and alligator, deer, and bird hunters were drawn to the wildlife. In the ensuing years the canals have silted over and the river of grass has been reestablished.

Keep east past the campsite, where the path makes a slight jog to the south at mile 4.7, before resuming its easterly tack at mile 5.1. Cypress trees increase in number and the trailside vegetation thickens. These cypress trees shade the area and allow more luxuriant growth of trees such as gumbo-limbo.

Pass another monitoring station at mile 5.5. A few pines show up on the far side of the canal at mile 7.1. Limestone rocks occasionally lie beside the water and make for good resting benches. There are more tall cypress domes, including one exceeding sixty feet high at mile 8.1. Cypress domes are also known as tree islands, but hammocks are dry tree islands. Peer into the wet woods and look for epiphytes on the trunks of the cypresses.

Palms become more abundant along the road. Look for the numerous tree islands to your left. At mile 9.6, pass a canoe that is used by park personnel to cross to the north side of the canal. There are no paddles here—they pull themselves across the ten-foot-wide waterway with a metal cable strung across the water. Watch for worn patches of ground leading into the canal. This is where alligators enter and exit the water. Don't be surprised if you see a 'gator lying across the old roadway.

At mile 10.0, pass an old road leading left. This roadway is long grown over and impassable. At mile 10.5, come to the Old Ingraham campsite and the end of the trail. There is a water monitoring station here, too. To your south are good prairie views. Beyond this, the Old Ingraham Highway has been leveled and the excess soil dumped back in the canal to restore the natural flow of water through the Everglades.

Otter Cave Trail

Begin: Shark Valley Visitor Center
End: Shark Valley Visitor Center
Distance: 1.2-mile roundtrip
Trail Difficulty: Moderate
Highlights: Scenic pools, wildlife, solution holes
Hazards: Solution holes, alligators, mosquitoes
Trail Connections: Bobcat Boardwalk
Season: Fall–spring
Maps: Everglades National Park map
Trailhead: From the intersection of Krome Avenue (SR 997) and the Tamiami Trail (US 41) at the entrance to the Miccosukee reservation, drive 18 miles west. The entrance is on the left. The park is open from 8:30 a.m. to 6:00 p.m. There is a car entrance fee; your receipt is good for entrance at any other unit of Everglades National Park for one week.

Complementing Shark Valley's popular bike and tram trail and Bobcat Boardwalk, the Otter Cave Trail gets you out into the Everglades at a walking pace, where you'll see much more wildlife. Although the park considers the Otter Cave Trail to include the paved access to it, the natural trail is very short but very beautiful. It is frequently flooded, so check at the visitor center before you start your journey.

Walk behind the visitor center and follow the paved trail paralleling the canal. In spring, look carefully for newly hatched alligators and young waterfowl. On both sides of the pavement, the canals provide a never-ending show of wildlife. This narrow paved road was built in the early 1940s for oil exploration in the Everglades.

After 0.6 mile you reach the trailhead for the Otter Cave Trail on the left. Enter the tunnel of tropical vegetation—sparser now due to the ravages of Hurricane Wilma—and cross over a clear flowing stream with several pools. This is a scenic spot where wildlife gathers. Look for baby alligators and wading birds. When I visited, a young fluffy-feathered red-shouldered hawk was learning to fly. The footpath becomes a flat rocky surface underfoot. Notice and be cautious of the many small solution holes. Some of them are rather deep. Look down into them and see how they form a Swiss-cheese network of passageways right under your feet. This is the bedrock of the Everglades, allowing water to flow within a protected aquifer just below the surface. There is one large hole right in front of the bench.

The trail curves to the right, passing under more tropical hammock trees. It skirts a large cypress tree with knees poking out of the footpath. You are paralleling a narrow natural waterway to your right. Notice the change in pitch of the water as it drops down small shelves of rock—tiny rapids. The more natural trail ends all too soon, emerging at the paved section. Don't be surprised to see a large alligator guarding the culvert that directs the natural stream into the canal. Turn right. You reach the trailhead again at 0.8 mile. Continue walking along the pavement back to the visitor center to complete the hike.

Pa-Hay-Okee Boardwalk

Begin: Main Park Road
End: Main Park Road
Distance: 0.2-mile loop
Trail Difficulty: Wheelchair accessible
Highlights: Vast vista of the river of grass
Hazards: Mosquitoes
Trail Connections: None
Season: Year-round
Maps: Everglades National Park map
Trailhead: From the Ernest Coe Visitor Center, follow Main Park Road for 10.5 miles to the Pa-Hay-Okee turnoff on the right. Drive 1.3 miles down the side road to the parking area.

Figure 5. The River of Grass extends to the horizon at Pa-Hay-Okee. Photo by Sandra Friend

Pa-Hay-Okee is the Seminole name for "River of Grass," the name Marjorie Stoneman Douglas bestowed on the Everglades while advocating to have the region protected as a national park. This trail is a short boardwalk with a tall observation tower. Both provide a close-up look at the river of grass.

Start at the boardwalk entrance on the right and follow the boardwalk out into the sawgrass prairie. Look straight down and you can see the same jagged karst bedrock that was in the pine rocklands, complete with solution holes filled with water and aquatic plants, but here the rock is host to sawgrass. The sawgrass prairie stretches on forever, broken only by tree islands in the distance.

Ascend the staircase to the observation tower, which is surrounded by cypress trees and stands atop a small tree island with dense cocoplum in the understory. From this shady perch, you can see incredible vistas across the prairie. Look straight down to see more water-filled solution holes. They are often the only water source for wildlife during the dry season.

A boardwalk ramp, which is wheelchair accessible, leads you through the cypress canopy and back down to the forest floor. The trail ends at the end of the parking area.

Pine Land Trail

Begin: Main Park Road
End: Main Park Road
Distance: 0.4-mile loop
Trail Difficulty: Wheelchair accessible
Highlights: Pine rocklands habitat, solution holes
Hazards: Trailside solution holes, mosquitoes
Trail Connections: None
Season: Year-round
Maps: Everglades National Park map
Trailhead: From the Ernest Coe Visitor Center, follow Main Park Road for 4.4 miles to the Pine Land Trail turnoff on the right. Walk up to the canopied bench and interpretive sign where the trail begins.

Long Pine Key is an island in the Everglades with the largest remaining pine rockland forest in Florida. Once a common habitat all over Southeast Florida, these rocky pine forests were dynamited and bulldozed to build farms and later cities. Their slender pines, a subspecies of slash pine called Dade County pine, are highly resistant to rot and insects and were prized for building structures. The Pine Land Trail offers a short walk through this rare habitat.

Keep right at the fork to follow the interpretive markers in order. The path meanders through the forest, where saw palmetto dominates the understory. Notice the many deep solution holes adjoining the trail. In some cases they are so close to the pavement that boards have been installed to prevent an errant footfall. There is one enormous and deep solution hole on the right that is the size of a small swimming pool. In addition to the slender pines—many of which are at odd angles, having had their root balls lifted up during hurricanes—there are many poisonwood trees here. Continue around the loop to complete your hike at the entrance kiosk.

Rowdy Bend Trail

Begin: Main Park Road
End: Snake Bight Trail
Distance: 2.8 miles one way
Trail Difficulty: Moderate
Highlights: Immersion in the coastal prairie habitat
Hazards: Mosquitoes, mud
Trail Connections: Snake Bight Trail
Season: Winter
Maps: Everglades National Park map
Trailhead: From the Flamingo Visitor Center, follow Main Park Road north for 2.7 miles to the Rowdy Bend trailhead on the right.

The Everglades are no stranger to hurricanes, which shape landscape and habitat on a grand scale. The unique coastal prairie habitats of the Everglades are ever changing, a battle of wills between salt-loving and salt-intolerant species. Made up of marl mud thrown up into slightly higher elevations during hurricane storm surges, they support vast fields of succulent-like saltwort (*Batis maritime*) introduced to me as "pickle-weed" on a ranger-led hike during the 1960s. The thick shiny leaves taste briny when chewed. Battling for the open prairie are spartina grasses and buttonwood, a member of the mangrove family. Neither appreciates the influx of salty marl that a hurricane storm surge brings. And so the current score stands: saltwort 1, buttonwood 0.

The Rowdy Bend Trail showcases the coastal prairie in a way that won't leave you fighting to extract your shoes from the mud, as can happen on the Coastal Prairie Trail. Connecting to the Snake Bight Trail, Rowdy Bend Trail provides an alternate (and in my opinion, more scenic) route to access the boardwalk at Snake Bight to watch for flamingos in winter. You can combine the two trails and the Main Park Road to make a long loop day hike of 7.6 miles. Bikes are permitted on the trail, but it's a narrow track only suitable for mountain bikes.

Starting at the trailhead, follow the Rowdy Bend Trail down the remnants of an old paved road. As down on the Coastal Prairie Trail, cotton pickers in the 1930s targeted the coastal prairies along Snake Bight to eradicate wild cotton (which still exists here, and is now an endangered species with showy flowers). The trail partially follows the old cotton-picking roads. Just 0.3 miles into the hike you reach your first open coastal prairie on the right edge of the trail; the footpath becomes sticky but solid marl before entering a tight corridor flanked by tropical forest—blolly, mahogany, gumbo-limbo, and cabbage palm host cascades of yellow nickerbean.

The dead, bleached bones of trees are the remains of buttonwoods that overloaded on the temporary intrusion of salt water into their habitat. A tangle of a stranger fig emerges from its host, the cabbage palm, before the trail curves left. You pass the remnants of faded trail signs at 1.1 miles; the trail becomes a deep rut in the prairie grass, with the broad prairie stretching off to your left. Bromeliads cling to what is left of the silent buttonwoods. A soft carpet of salt hay cushions your footfalls before the footpath becomes cementlike marl again.

Entering a buttonwood thicket at 1.5 miles, the trail passes a large prickly pear cactus poking out of the saltwort. The trail changes character and becomes more tropical as it curves past a small brackish pond off to the right, where bromeliads drape from buttonwood limbs. You reach another coastal prairie at 2.1 miles, where the thin jointed pipes of glasswort, another salt-loving plant, emerge between the crowds of saltwort. Stands of sea oxeye lend a dash of bright yellow to the landscape. The Rowdy Bend Trail rises up to end at the Snake Bight Trail at 2.8 miles. Turn right to walk out to the boardwalk and observation deck on Snake Bight (a roundtrip of 0.8 mile), turn left to follow the Snake Bight Trail to the Main Park Road (a 2-mile walk), or return the way you came.

Sandfly Island Nature Trail

Begin: Sandfly Island
End: Sandfly Island
Distance: 1.0-mile loop
Trail Difficulty: Easy
Highlights: Old homestead, spring
Hazards: Insects
Trail Connections: None
Season: Winter
Maps: Sandfly Island handout
Trailhead: This trail is accessible only by boat from the Gulf Coast Ranger Station, which lies in the northern part of the Everglades National Park, abutting Everglades City.

Hikers need a boat to access this large shell mound that was first home to Calusa Indians and later to white settlers. Sandfly Island is just a few miles west of the Gulf Coast Ranger Station, where there is a handout giving boating directions to the island. Once here, hikers can enjoy a loop trail that circles Sandfly.

After boating to the island, leave the Sandfly Island dock and immediately pass the cistern, foundation, and spring of the Boggess family. They once farmed the island, cultivating more than thirty acres of tomatoes. They arrived here in 1912. As you walk the island, think of this as your permanent home, with no modern conveniences like electricity and sparse contact with the outside world. Imagine what the Boggess family would think of their "back of beyond" if they could see it today.

The nature trail splits; take the left fork. The hammock forest here is rich with gumbo-limbo, poisonwood, and strangler fig. Mangrove drapes low-lying areas. Look for telltale tamarind trees that indicate another dwelling site. Tamarinds were often planted around homes. Swing around to the west side of the island, gaining glimpses of the water beyond Sandfly. Watch for a strangler fig engulfing a cabbage palm right on the path. The final feature of the trail is a boardwalk that extends over a creek and beneath a tall mangrove forest just before completing the loop.

Snake Bight Trail

Begin: Main Park Road
End: Snake Bight Overlook
Distance: 1.8 miles one way
Trail Difficulty: Easy
Highlights: Possibility of spotting flamingos in winter
Hazards: Mosquitoes, poisonwood
Trail Connections: Rowdy Bend Trail
Season: Winter
Maps: Everglades National Park map
Trailhead: From the Flamingo Visitor Center, follow Main Park Road north for 5.4 miles to the Snake Bight trailhead on the right.

Of the longer trails at Flamingo, Snake Bight has always been the most popular. You'll see cars jockeying for trailhead parking space along the Main Park Road during the winter season, when a handful of the area's namesakes return from the Yucatan to sift through the muck of Florida Bay and provide a "wow" moment for folks who hike and bike this easy linear route the 1.8 miles out to the observation deck. Bring strong binoculars, as the flock of flamingos—diminished in size greatly from a century ago—is often seen on distant mud flats, rarely up close.

Built as a road to reach the E. C. Knight Fish Company Processing Plant on Snake Bight, a sheltered bight inside Florida Bay, the Snake Bight Trail leads you along a straight, wide path of limestone spoil from the adjacent canal, built (as most were in this area) to drain the swamps. A forest of black and red mangroves flanks the canal, and the higher ground provided by building the road has been taken over by tall tropical trees. Most of them lost their dense upper branches to Hurricane Wilma, which stripped away the shady walk that most visitors appreciated—but nature will heal and the shade will return. You'll recognize the peeling bark of the gumbo-limbo and the sinuous base of the strangler fig. And perhaps you'll recognize a tree worth avoiding—the poisonwood. Like poison ivy, it is a member of the cashew family, but it packs a toxic punch ten times the strength of poison ivy if you get its sap on you by rubbing into its leaves or leaning against the oozing dark spots on its trunk. In Everglades National Park, it is common. Don't touch a tree you don't know.

At 0.7 mile, you pass a cotton pickers' road on the left that leads to Crocodile Point. Don't go there. Not because of the endangered American crocodiles that make these shores their home—ask at the Flamingo marina where you can see them—but because the old road leads right into a stand of manchineel trees. If you think poisonwood sounds bad, manchineel is worse. Its sap is corrosive—and water won't cut it. The tree oozes sap, it spurts sap if cut, the fruits are deadly, and supposedly you should not stand under these trees when it rains. According to the State of Florida, it "causes severe dermatitis." In Florida the manchineel is an endangered species, found only here and in the tropical hammocks of the Keys.

On the far side of the canal you begin to see the coastal prairie habitat as you breathe in the salty tang of Florida Bay. Surrounded by their fingerlike protrusions called pneumatophores, black mangroves are the most common inhabitants of the mangrove forest. Look up, and you'll spot orchids and cactus in the trees. At 1.4 miles, you reach the unmarked entrance to the Rowdy Bend Trail, a broad break in the trees to the right. Continue straight ahead. Off to the right is a broad, open marl prairie broken by stands of black mangrove. The old road ends at an old auto turnaround close to where the E. G. Knight Fish Company Processing Plant stood in the early 1940s. Fishermen back then used Snake Bight Canal to bring their catch to Main Park Road, which was then known as the Ingraham Highway.

Just past the turnaround at 1.8 miles, the boardwalk begins. It breaks out of the woods and crosses the mud flats to overlook Snake Bight. If the mosquitoes aren't bad—and be warned, they will be deadly intense after any rainfall, at any time of year—take some time to enjoy the view. Get those binoculars out and see if you are lucky enough to spot the flamingos or other wading birds that canvass the shallows at this time of year.

Hiking Trails of
Big Cypress National Preserve

The Big Cypress is Florida's least used and least appreciated federal land. I did not explore it extensively until after nearly a decade of enjoying Florida's natural resources. The "big" in Big Cypress refers to the size of the swamp, not necessarily to the size of the cypress trees, though pockets of the ancient giants still exist. The Big Cypress adjoins the north side of the Everglades National Park, sporting over 700,000 acres of cypress sloughs, pinelands, tropical hammocks, and freshwater marshes.

The Florida Trail starts its northward journey here, and it starts off with a bang. The trail here is rough, rugged, and remote, while passing through some incredible scenery. Have you ever walked through a dwarf cypress swamp? Here the FT leaves Loop Road and wastes no time in initiating hikers into "swamp slogging" through picturesque cypress sloughs, and crossing Roberts Lakes Strand, where water is far more extensive than dry land, eventually meeting the Tamiami Trail.

The FT continues north beyond the Tamiami Trail. Wet feet are the norm here, too. Hikers must contend with crossing muddy swamp-buggy roads. But this inconvenience is well worth the views. And how could you expect not to get your feet wet in the Big Cypress Swamp? It is not all watery, though; cypress sloughs often give way to pine islands and prairies, offering continually changing landscapes. These pine islands allow camping possibilities and are also habitat for deer. And where there are deer, there is the Florida panther, for deer is its preferred fare. The panther needs remoteness, too, and the Big Cypress has plenty of that, especially as you continue north on the Florida Trail. Tree islands become lusher, with palms and eventually tropical trees, such as gumbo-limbo and Simpson stopper. In the far north of the preserve, cypress trees once again dominate, and these tree islands act as dry waysides for resting and camping.

During the 1800s it was in this expanse that is now the Big Cypress where the Seminoles hid away, outfoxing U.S. troops until the federals gave up. Backpackers find that the trip on the Florida Trail from Tamiami Trail to Interstate Highway 75 is unique, and they soon understand why the Seminoles chose the Big Cypress to make their last stand.

Florida Trail, Loop Road to Tamiami Trail

Begin: Loop Road
End: Tamiami Trail, US 41
Distance: 7.8 miles
Trail Difficulty: Difficult
Highlights: Cypress swamps, isolation
Hazards: Inundated path, irregular limestone footing, deep cypress domes
Trail Connections: Florida Trail, Tamiami Trail to Thirteen Mile Camp
Season: Winter
Maps: Florida Trail Big Cypress South, Big Cypress National Preserve map
Trailhead: From the Oasis Visitor Center at Big Cypress National Preserve take US 41, Tamiami Trail, east for 14.8 miles to Loop Road. Turn right on Loop Road and follow it for 13.5 miles to the Florida Trail, which starts on your right. Look for a small kiosk and an orange-blazed track leading north into cypress swamp.

This is the wettest and possibly most unusual path in this guidebook. It leaves Loop Road, which is the southern terminus of the entire Florida Trail, and heads north through a nearly continuous bald cypress woodland that is underwater most of the year, including during the drier winter hiking season. Even at the best of times this section of the Florida Trail is inundated for 50 percent of its distance, and that may extend to 95 percent. Prepare for wet feet along the entire trail and possibly water to your knees at times. Before hiking this section of the Florida Trail, call Big Cypress Preserve at (239) 695-1201 and check on water levels. The trail is marked at 1-mile intervals from Loop Road all the way to I-75 with signs that also give GPS coordinates.

All this wetness may seem daunting. On the other hand, it demystifies swamps to a degree: you will be hiking through one. The path also passes through sawgrass prairies, past tree islands, and through Robert Lakes Strand, where the towering cypresses covered in air plants and ferns, mixed with tropical hammocks and clear flowing water, offer a wild Florida landscape.

Figure 6. Johnny Molloy at the Florida Trail south terminus on Loop Road. Photo by Barb Haapala

Head north from Loop Road and immediately drop into a bald cypress forest that will most likely be wet. The water below you is clear and harbors much aquatic life. The cypress trees soon grow tall. Pocked limestone makes for irregular footing—watch your step. Occasional slash pines are on higher spots. Keep an eye peeled for the orange blazes identifying the trail route, as animal paths sometimes cross the FT.

At mile 1.1 pass a small tree island on your right, then enter a sawgrass prairie with scattered small cypress. At mile 2.0, pass a pine island on your right before coming to a larger pine-palm hammock on your right at mile 2.4. This one may have dry ground and potential camping or sitting spots. Return to open prairie, which melds into cypress woods with an understory of sawgrass. Pines stay to your right with occasional tree islands scattered among the cypress.

Emerge into a pine-palm hammock at mile 3.3. This is Frog Hammock. To the left of the trail is a campsite with dry ground, fire ring, and a defunct pump well. Other artifacts from old hunting camps lie on the periphery. Frog Hammock is your best bet for camping between Loop Road and Tamiami Trail. Leave the hammock and reenter a sawgrass prairie. Once again cypress trees slowly increase in size and number. This increase peaks out in a tall cypress stand. Watch for a sharp right turn in the center of the stand. Leave the bald cypress and follow the path as it "climbs" to higher ground and a full-blown hardwood hammock, heavy with ferns. The dense flora and often saturated soil are not favorable for camping.

Abruptly the trail drops down into a cypress swamp. Here clumps of dry ground, rich with vegetation, alternate with clear moving water from which widely buttressed cypresses emerge. You are crossing the Roberts Lakes Strand. Stay with the blazes here as the trail veers left and begins to follow an old logging tram road due west at mile 5.2.

The old tram road passes alongside cypress trees until mile 5.6, where the westerly course abruptly turns north, to the right, still in medium-sized cypress. The trail is poorly marked here. At mile 6.8, the cypress woods thicken and the water correspondingly deepens. You are in a cypress dome, an area where the trees stand taller than others on the horizon and resemble a dome. Pass through a second cypress dome, then the trailside woods gradually thin out to a sawgrass prairie before reaching Tamiami Trail and the Oasis Visitor Center at mile 7.8. The Florida Trail continues across Tamiami Trail, crossing the northern Big Cypress Preserve before ending at I-75 after 30 miles.

Florida Trail, Tamiami Trail to Thirteen Mile Camp

Begin: Tamiami Trail
End: Thirteen Mile Camp
Distance: 16.8 miles
Trail Difficulty: Difficult
Highlights: Cypress sloughs, pine islands, wildlife, isolation, navigational challenge
Hazards: Wet hiking, poorly marked trail
Trail Connections: Florida Trail, Loop Road to Tamiami Trail; Florida Trail, Thirteen Mile Camp to I-75
Season: Winter
Maps: Florida Trail Big Cypress South, Big Cypress National Preserve map
Trailhead: This section of the Florida Trail starts at the Oasis Visitor Center at Big Cypress National Preserve on US 41, 21 miles east of Everglades City from the junction of US 41 and CR 29.

This hike traverses some of the most rugged terrain in Florida, the Big Cypress National Preserve. It passes through wet cypress sloughs, sawgrass prairies, and pine islands covered in palmetto. This is also the habitat of the endangered Florida panther. Numerous birds and deer also call the Big Cypress home. The hike is best enjoyed as an overnight backpack, as the distances are prohibitive for all but an abbreviated thereand-back day hike. There are numerous campsites to pitch your tent, and combining this section of the Florida Trail with the FT section from Thirteen Mile Camp to I-75 can make for a grand and rugged multiday backpacking trip.

The hiking is challenging; wet feet and slogging through water up to your knees are guaranteed. The sun can be brutal in open areas. And following the orange blazes of the often faint trail takes a keen eye and patience. It is far more than thirteen miles to Thirteen Mile Camp, which is a good destination. Be prepared when you enter the Big Cypress.

Some folks who visit this area drive "swamp buggies." These contraptions look like Jeeps on steroids, with their oversized tires and elevated frames. They make wide muddy paths, which you will cross. Your trip via foot power will give you a unique experience, very unlike hiking anywhere else in the United States.

Start your hike by leaving the west end of the Oasis Visitor Center and following the orange-blazed Florida Trail between two fences along a canal. Soon turn right, still following the fence line on an elevated roadbed that borders an air strip to your right. Begin heading north, the primary direction for the hike. There is a sawgrass prairie to your left.

At 0.4 mile, make the first of several swamp buggy trail crossings. Palm and cypress trees border the trail. Come to your first pine island at 1.0 mile. The path is drier here. Overhead tall slash pines shade palms and palmettos. There are occasional hardwood hammocks scattered among the evergreens.

Watch your footing over the mud and pocked limestone as cypress trees become more prevalent. Watch also for the markings for the Florida Trail, which can be standard orange-painted blazes on trees or orange flagging tape tied around trees. The trail begins to alternate between drier pine-palm hammocks and wet cypress-sawgrass complexes.

At mile 3.0, after a plethora of swamp buggy trails, come to the blue-blazed Blue Loop, leaving to the left. This side trail has been permanently abandoned. Stay forward on the Florida Trail, as it keeps north through increasing palms and hardwoods broken by occasional cypress sloughs.

At mile 5.0, the trail steps over limestone pocked with particularly deep holes, often filled with water. The terrain open onto a cypress slough then you emerge into pineland, where exotic melaleuca trees have been cut down. Perhaps you can see their fallen trunks. These invaders are identified by their paperlike white bark. Originally from Australia, melaleucas were brought to Florida as border-forming ornamental trees. They prefer wet or moist areas. This tree is also the subject of an urban legend: that melaleuca trees are so widespread because a greedy land speculator spread their seeds by airplane in order to dry and then develop the many wetlands in South Florida. No matter their origin, melaleucas are considered one of the Sunshine State's worst invaders, being nearly impossible to eradicate.

At mile 6.2, just to the right of the trail in a pine, palm, and palmetto area, is Seven Mile Camp. It may be marked by a sign. The camp is

Figure 7. Backpackers swamp-slog through dwarf pond cypress forest. Photo by Johnny Molloy

shaded by wax myrtle and has a fire ring, sitting logs, and a pocked limestone hole filled with water. Water can also be found in a cypress dome, an area of tall cypresses that usually indicates deeper water. One such dome, and an alternative water source, is located west of the camp.

Keep north past Seven Mile Camp, and at 6.4 miles pass the blue-blazed westward shortcut to the Blue Loop. This shortcut is also neglected and closed. Past this, the footbed of the Florida Trail becomes fainter—keep your eyes on the orange blazes as the trail passes through mixed pine and cypress areas. Many of the cypress trees you pass are below head level and crowd the trail. The vegetation in this flat land changes with the slightest changes in elevation.

At mile 9.6, you come to an exceptionally large and wide pine island. The slash pines overhead are noticeably tall. Soon there is a pile of limestone rocks on the trail. This is Ten Mile Camp, which may be marked with a sign. Stay northeasterly and once again dive into cypress. Keep alternating between cypress and pine, until entering an extended cypress strand at mile 11.1, now heading northwesterly. Before, the predominant pinelands were bridged by cypress sloughs. Now, predominant cypress sloughs are bridged by sporadic pinelands.

At mile 12.0 the trail circles around an immense prairie of head-high sawgrass to your left. Leave the tall sawgrass and head through mixed landscape of prairies, cypress woods, and pine islands. At mile 14.6, come to the northern terminus of the blue-blazed and abandoned Blue Loop. The Florida Trail turns sharply right here, to the north, heading into open pine woods. This end of the Blue Loop is even more remote and poorly marked than the previous junctions and may well be missed by most hikers.

Follow the orange blazes through pine islands, cypress sloughs, and sawgrass prairies. Palms become more prevalent on drier lands. Briefly pass through thick, tall sawgrass near palm trees at mile 15.5. Keep a constant watch for the orange blazes. At mile 16.8, enter the hammock of Thirteen Mile Camp. Even from a distance, this tree island is lusher than those previously passed. It features a profusion of cabbage palms and such hardwood hammock species as live oak. The sure signs of being at Thirteen Mile Camp are the broken-down handpump well in the hammock's center and a trail register. This is an excellent campsite. Water can be obtained from a nearby cypress dome. From here, it is 14.2 miles north on the Florida Trail to I-75.

Florida Trail, Thirteen Mile Camp to I-75

Begin: Thirteen Mile Camp
End: I-75
Distance: 13.1 miles
Trail Difficulty: Difficult
Highlights: Tropical hardwood hammocks, solitude, cypress sloughs
Hazards: Swamp walking, isolation, poorly marked trail
Trail Connections: Florida Trail, Tamiami Trail to Thirteen Mile Camp; Florida Trail, I-75 to Seminole Reservation
Season: Winter
Maps: Florida Trail Big Cypress North, Big Cypress National Preserve map
Trailhead: The south trailhead can only be reached by foot from Tamiami Trail, but the north terminus can be accessed at the main rest stop on the "Alligator Alley" portion of I-75.

This section of the Florida Trail is very remote and rugged. It passes through the northern part of the Big Cypress National Preserve. As elsewhere noted, the "big" in Big Cypress refers to the size of the 700,000-acre swamp, not the size of the trees, and after this walk you will understand the meaning of the word. The trail is characterized by miles and miles of poorly marked cypress sloughs, punctuated by slash pine–sabal palm hammocks and rich tropical hardwood hammocks. Some swamp buggy trails do pass through here; however, if you are looking for a first-rate wilderness experience, this section of the Florida Trail combined with the section from Oasis Visitor Center to Thirteen Mile Camp is the wildest walking in South Florida. A hike through the Big Cypress clearly reveals why this area is one of the last strongholds of the Florida panther.

Start this portion of the Florida Trail by heading north out of Thirteen Mile Camp, an excellent overnighting spot shaded by palms, pines, and live oaks. Cross a swamp buggy road and enter a cypress slough. Soon start a pattern of walking sloughs and crossing palm-pine lands. Though the trail makes many twists and turns, it keeps a generally northward course. More abrupt turns are marked with double orange blazes. At

Figure 8. Ivy Camp is a welcome dry spot in the wet Big Cypress National Preserve. Photo by Johnny Molloy

mile 1.5, pass a prairie dotted with stumps of cypress and pine that were sawn. Soon, walk by two bamboo stands in succession. Simply put, the trail is hard to follow here. As soon as you lose the trail, backtrack immediately to the last blaze or flagging tape you saw and then reorient until you find the next blaze. *Do not continue without finding blazes.*

Cypress woods become more dominant, with numerous tall domes on the horizon. At mile 2.6, come to a barbed-wire fence on your left. Walk alongside the fence for 0.2 mile, then turn away from the fence, now heading north. At mile 3.3, make an abrupt left turn off a swamp buggy road the trail has picked up. Enter a pine-palm hammock but soon slog through more sloughs. Come alongside a rich tropical hammock on your left at mile 3.7. Live oak, ferns, cocoplum, and more make a shady and dry resting spot. Soon pass two more rich hammocks.

Continue north through a sea of cypress dotted with small tree islands, just high enough to support dry land species such as cabbage palm. The swamp deepens before coming to a large, especially rich tropical hammock on your right at mile 5.2. This is Oak Hill Camp, which has tall live oak, palms, gumbo-limbo, Simpson stoppers, and other lush vegetation. A path has been cut to the center of the hammock, where there is a campsite. The year-round growing season can quickly obliterate camps, but this hammock has been a traditional camping spot.

Beyond this hammock, the swamp deepens again; you can expect water to your knees or higher, with next to no land or resting spots save for a semblance of land near the trail at 7.3 miles. Pass smaller tree islands on the horizon. Keep north, then northwesterly through mostly cypress for quite a distance, though the pine-palm and sawgrass prairie ecosystems are represented. Finally, the trail comes to Ivy Camp at 9.4 miles. Ivy Camp is a small but decidedly high piece of land that is a campsite. Beyond Ivy Camp, the trail crosses and joins buggy roads. Keep slogging through cypress of differing sizes, shapes, and forms, with bigger cypress growing in deeper water.

By mile 11.7, palm islands appear on a sawgrass horizon. Step onto dry ground at mile 11.6. Enjoy dry footing in the pine-palm lands, then make an abrupt right turn to the east and come to the main buggy road connecting to I-75 at mile 11.9. Turn left and follow the wide, muddy trail north before coming to a high metal fence with a gate at mile 12.9. Walk through the gate and turn left, going against the flow of an on-ramp to I-75. Walk 0.4 mile to the I-75 rest area, ending your hike at mile 13.3. Here are phones, water, and soft drink machines, quite a change from the wild Big Cypress. The Florida Trail continues under the interstate overpass and heads north to reach the Big Cypress Indian Reservation in 7.6 miles.

Florida Trail, I-75 to Big Cypress Indian Reservation

Begin: I-75 rest area
End: Big Cypress Indian Reservation
Distance: 7.6 miles
Trail Difficulty: Moderate
Highlights: Vast forests, loop hike possibilities
Hazards: Florida panther habitat
Trail Connections: Florida Trail, Thirteen Mile Camp to I-75
Maps: Florida Trail Big Cypress North, Big Cypress National Preserve map
Trailhead: The south end of this section can be reached by taking I-75 across Alligator Alley to reach the main rest area between Naples and Fort Lauderdale. The north access is restricted because it ends at the Big Cypress Indian Reservation boundary.

This part of the Florida Trail is a completely different experience than the rest of the Big Cypress portion. Here the FT leaves the busy I-75 rest area and heads north into woods and swamps following Nobles Road, an elevated grade with paralleling canals, where alligators sun in large numbers. The elevated roadbed makes for dry hiking and much more efficient passage than the swamp slogging of the lower Big Cypress. The track passes pine islands, palm forests, and live oak woodland. It also passes amidst Brazilian pepper, which is slowly but surely being eradicated in the Big Cypress. The trail travels along areas of former human habitation, where you can see the old Nobles homesite, foundations of a slaughterhouse (this was once a major cattle area), and also an airstrip. The Nobles designated backcountry campsite is located by the old airstrip. Before leaving the Big Cypress, the FT joins Jones Grade, also an elevated track, and follows it to the reservation line. The 8.5-mile trail with which it forms a loop features three designated backcountry campsites, making backpack trips of up to 15 miles up here in the Big Cypress's "Far North" a cinch.

To begin this portion of trail from the I-75 rest stop, head east toward the underpass access, reaching the north side of the interstate. From here, turn right again, eastbound and heading toward the oncoming traffic of the access ramp for 200 yards. Look left for a gate that may looked locked but isn't. Pass through the gate and join Nobles Road, a raised roadbed closed to vehicles except those of Big Cypress personnel. Keep forward, shortly coming to a Y-intersection at 0.4 mile. Here, veer left at a trail registration box. A canal lies to the left of the road, dug for fill to raise the road. Alligators are often seen sunning themselves along the canal. Palm hammocks, cypress domes, and pine islands character- ize the flora, which generally favors drier species than the Big Cypress south of I-75.

At 1.1 miles, reach the southern junction with the blue-blazed loop that reconnects with the Florida Trail at its northern end. The FT contin- ues forward along Nobles Road. The trailside landscape here will change over time. What once were impenetrable Brazilian pepper thickets will become more open and return to a more Floridian landscape. The crushed and packed rock track makes for easy open hiking, but it can be hard on the feet. Look for old bridges that leave to your left, spanning the canal to access lands to the west. Hikers seeking solitude can cross these bridges and explore deeper into the Big Cypress. Notice a trail leading right, which makes for a shortcut across to the blue-blazed loop trail to the east.

At 5.0 miles, the main trail makes a hard turn to the east at the old Nobles homesite and airstrip. This is also the end of the canal to your left. A pond is near this turn as well. Just ahead, the Nobles backcountry campsite is located on the edge of the field to your left, part of the old airstrip. Notice the relics here.

Beyond the airstrip, the trail passes large live oaks and palms aplenty before reaching Jones Grade at 5.8 miles. This is the north end of the blue-blazed loop. Here, the FT turns left, westbound, and passes the concrete foundation of a cattle slaughter house at 6.1 miles. The elevated track passes through mixed woods with pine predominance before reaching the gate at the Big Cypress Seminole Indian Reservation at 7.6 miles. From here, you must be a Florida Trail Association member and have written permission from the reservation to continue north on the Florida Trail.

Fire Prairie Trail

Begin: Turner River Road
End: Oil drilling pad
Distance: 2.5 miles one way
Trail Difficulty: Easy
Highlights: Broad views of sawgrass prairie
Hazards: Mosquitoes, lightning
Trail Connections: None
Season: Year-round
Maps: Big Cypress National Preserve map
Trailhead: From Everglades City, drive north on CR 29 for 3 miles to US 41, Tamiami Trail. Turn right on US 41 and head east for 6.7 miles to Turner River Road (CR 839) at the H. P. Williams Wayside. Turn left on Turner River Road and follow it north for 14.4 miles to the Fire Prairie trailhead on your left.

This footpath explores the far western reaches of the Big Cypress National Preserve. It follows a raised roadbed through a cypress swamp and open sawgrass prairie to end at the site of an old oil derrick. Florida's first oil well was drilled during the 1920s in nearby Sunniland, and the Barron Collier family still has live wells in other locations, as they own the mineral rights beneath the preserve. Now all that remains here is a dry path to a sawgrass prairie with extensive views. The soundscape out here is a major attraction. Birds can be heard from quite a distance over the open sawgrass. The trail's name comes from the regularity with which the ecosystem burns. A healthy sawgrass prairie and attendant tree islands are maintained by fire at regular intervals.

Leave Turner River Road, heading west on a raised roadbed. A canal runs alongside the roadbed, flanked by a cypress strand dense with bromeliads. Ferns crowd the sides of the footpath, which has a fair amount of shade. After 0.3 mile, a divergent roadbed extends to the north; keep walking straight ahead.

The trail opens up to the sawgrass prairie, which is dotted with islands of cypress, cedar, and pines. Look for the blackened trunks of the trees on the wooded islands, testament to fire's presence on the sawgrass

Figure 9. Blooming bromeliad, or air plant, is a fascinating component of many South Florida paths, like the Fire Prairie Trail. Photo by Johnny Molloy

prairie. Lightning strikes during the rainy season set off natural burns. If the forest begins to creep off the islands and into the prairie, park personnel use prescribed burns to mimic the acts of nature.

The margins of the roadbed are covered in high grass, but you can still enjoy extensive views to the southwest and north. Look for butterfly weed and swamp lily in the prairie, and little blue herons squawking and fussing in the high grass as you walk past. At 1.4 miles the trail curves to the right on the open prairie. After 2.5 miles, you arrive at an open, mown square field that looks oddly out of place on this wild landscape. The park service mows the trail and the pad, which is square and thus stands out more. A few scattered palm trees provide shade. This artificial bed is the site of an old oil derrick. It is now a good place to contemplate the beauty of the sawgrass prairies of the Big Cypress National Preserve.

Kirby Storter Wayside Boardwalk

Begin: Parking area at Tamiami Trail
End: Overlook along New River
Distance: 0.5 mile one way
Trail Difficulty: Wheelchair accessible
Highlights: Variety of habitats traversed
Hazards: Slippery when wet
Trail Connections: None
Season: Year-round
Maps: Big Cypress National Preserve map
Trailhead: From the intersection of SR 29 and US 41 north of Everglades City, drive east on US 41 (Tamiami Trail), passing park headquarters and the Turner River canoe put-in. This new trailhead is a prominent feature on the right before the New River and has composting toilets and picnic tables at the parking area.

Thanks to the efforts of the Friends of Big Cypress Preserve, the Kirby Storter Wayside Boardwalk is the preserve's first showcase of habitats that can be enjoyed by all ages and abilities at all times of year. It is a broad boardwalk, perfect for families to stroll together and wheelchair accessible as well. Starting off from the parking area, look out over the open prairie where small cypresses dot the landscape. The blooms of foxglove, rattlesnake master, and duck potato peer out from the needle rush. At 0.1 mile, you reach a large chickee—a historic Calusa and Seminole dwelling of thatched roof with open sides for breezes—with seating, a perfect place to relax and escape from summer rains. Along the curve just past the chickee, limestone studded with solution holes sits just under the surface of the water, with mats of periphyton strung across it. Carnivorous bladderworts float in the still water, providing mosquito control by absorbing mosquito larvae.

A rise in elevation at 0.3 mile means a change in habitat—here you see the trees of the floodplain forest, pop ash and red maple. Cabbage palms rise from small islands. Around the next bend there is another change in vegetation, with dense sword fern and marsh fern blanketing the understory, cocoplum showing off its inch-long fruits each fall, and even some strangler figs. The water becomes darker but still clear as the boardwalk winds into a cypress dome and then into a cypress slough at 0.3 mile, where the flow of the New River is visible. Cypresses tower overhead, forming deep shade. Look off to the left to see a gnarled pop ash with a virtual hanging garden of bromeliads clinging to its limbs. Off to the right, ferns define the edge of the river's shallows.

After 0.5 mile, the boardwalk ends at a large platform overlooking a mat of water hyacinths on the New River. Benches provide another resting place before you turn around and retrace your steps back to the parking area.

Tree Snail Hammock Interpretive Trail

Begin: Loop Road
End: Loop Road
Distance: 0.3 mile loop
Trail Difficulty: Easy
Highlights: Endangered tree snails
Hazards: Mosquitoes, poison ivy
Trail Connections: Florida Trail, Loop Road to Oasis, is just up the road
Season: Fall–spring
Maps: None
Trailhead: From the Tamiami Trail at Forty Mile Bend in the Miccosukee Reservation, turn south on Loop Road and follow it through Pinecrest until you see the Everglades Environmental Center on the left. Park at the center; the trail starts on the opposite side of the road.

In the late 1800s, it was all the rage to collect colorful tree snails of the genus *Liguus* from hammocks deep within the Everglades and Big Cypress. This short interpretive trail showcases the perfect habitat for these living works of art. Walk slowly and scan your surroundings. With sharp eyes, you'll spot the snails grazing on algae on smooth-barked trees such as Spanish stopper and Jamaica dogwood.

The trail stays in deep shade beneath a thick canopy of tropical forest. Watch your footing, as there are many surface outcrops of Miami limestone. About halfway through the hike, you walk through an outdoor classroom used by the environmental center. The benches surround the remains of a moonshine whiskey still that was operational back in 1881. Notice the lush sword ferns and limestone-loving spleenwort on the forest floor; look up, and you'll see an endangered whisk fern perching in the crook of a strangler fig. The loop ends all too soon, as you emerge from the cool dark hammock out onto Loop Road.

Hiking Trails of Canaveral National Seashore

Along a windswept barrier island, Canaveral National Seashore protects 58,000 acres of maritime hammocks, dunes, and coastline surrounding Cape Canaveral, a natural sandy cape that formed where ocean currents meet. The park was designated in 1975 and is uniquely located on the frost line, the northernmost point for many tropical plants, such as stopper and wild coffee, to thrive. Like the adjacent Merritt Island National Wildlife Refuge, it is a major stopover point for migratory birds in fall and spring. The park includes lands managed by NASA as a buffer zone for the Kennedy Space Center.

While the southern unit of the national seashore is a prime destination for beachgoers out of Titusville and Cocoa Beach, the quieter northern unit marks the end of the road south of New Smyrna Beach and Bethune Beach. It is here that you can explore the habitats and enjoy the views on a variety of trails.

At the northernmost end of the park, Turtle Mound is a distinct landscape feature that can be seen for miles by boaters. It's a massive pile of oyster shells discarded by Timucuan people as long ago as 400 A.D. A short interpretive trail takes you to the crest for some spectacular views.

Farther south along the island in the dense forests of Eldora, a former fishing village, the Eldora Hammock Trail showcases the uniqueness of the maritime hammock with insightful interpretive markers.

Castle Windy is the last stop for hikers, where a short trail connects the beach parking area and the Indian River Lagoon. Take a picnic lunch and walk out to the estuarine cove to enjoy the view.

Castle Windy Trail

Begin: Parking Area 3
End: Mosquito Lagoon
Distance: 0.3 mile
Trail Difficulty: Easy
Highlights: Maritime hammock and view of Mosquito Lagoon
Hazards: Insects, soft sand
Trail Connections: None
Season: Fall–spring
Maps: Canaveral National Seashore brochure
Trailhead: Drive south of the Canaveral National Seashore entrance and turn right into the parking pull-off for Turtle Mound.

At Canaveral National Seashore, Castle Windy is the only trail that takes you from the Atlantic Ocean to the Mosquito Lagoon. And yes, it is always windy here, except while you're sheltered in the protected shade of the maritime hammock. This linear trail climbs the hills of the barrier island's maritime hammock, ancient dunes now topped with red bay and marlberry, Simpson stopper and yaupon holly. Look for gopher tortoises and armadillos. The trail ends at a scenic cove along the Indian River Lagoon. A picnic bench provides a place to sit and enjoy the view, which takes in the sweep of the coastline in both directions. Return the way you came to complete your walk.

Eldora Hammock Trail

Begin: Eldora Road
End: Eldora Road
Distance: 0.5-mile loop
Trail Difficulty: Easy
Highlights: Dense maritime hammock with unique interpretive markers
Hazards: Poison ivy, mosquitoes
Trail Connections: None
Season: Year-round
Maps: Canaveral National Seashore brochure
Trailhead: Drive 1.4 miles south of the Canaveral National Seashore entrance, and turn right on Eldora Road. Follow it to the fourth parking lot on the right with the "Eldora Hammock" sign.

Prior to the establishment of Canaveral National Seashore, Eldora was a fishing village, established in 1877 along the Mosquito Lagoon. You can still visit the Eldora State House down a wheelchair-accessible path to the Eldora Village Historic Site, just north of this trail. Maritime hammocks are the high points of this windswept peninsula, and the Eldora Hammock is a fine example.

Start at the trailhead and walk into the shady hammock, where a canopy of red bay blocks the sun so that wild coffee, sparkleberry, and marlberry thrive. The trail is somewhat overgrown and wild. The forest has a dense, tropical feel, and resurrection fern wraps the red bay limbs. Take your time to enjoy the unique interpretive markers—a lot of thought and research went into the information provided here.

At 0.3 mile, the trail drops down into a corridor of silvery saw palmetto tinted by salt breezes. It's a spectacular sight. Continue through the dense understory and emerge back at the parking lot after 0.5 mile.

Turtle Mound Trail

Begin: Turtle Mound trailhead
End: Top of Turtle Mound
Distance: 0.1 mile
Trail Difficulty: Easy
Highlights: View from the top of the mound
Hazards: Steep boardwalk
Trail Connections: None
Season: Year-round
Maps: Canaveral National Seashore brochure
Trailhead: Drive 0.5 mile south of the Canaveral National Seashore entrance and turn right into the parking pull-off for Turtle Mound.

Figure 10. Turtle Mound offers some of the best views on the Atlantic coast. Photo by Sandra Friend

Along Florida's Atlantic Coast, the prominent feature of Turtle Mound has been a navigational aid for generations. It is an oyster shell midden rising thirty-five feet above the Mosquito Lagoon, an archeological site dating back to 800 A.D. The view from the top is unsurpassed in the central Atlantic region of Florida.

Hiking the Turtle Mound Trail takes you to the summit. This interpretive boardwalk trail is not wheelchair accessible beyond where it overlooks the Mosquito Lagoon, as it ascends at a steep pitch while entering the fragrant shade of a coastal hammock that has formed around and atop the 1.5 million bushels of oyster shells that the Timucua dropped on this spot. Turn right at the top to walk out on a deck overlooking both the Mosquito Lagoon and the bright blue of the Atlantic Ocean, the view reaching all the way north past Bethune Beach. Mounds of morning glory cover the sand atop the promontory. Off to the left is another viewing deck with different views of the lagoon and the ocean. Return via the steeply sloped boardwalk, and use the handrails if it is slippery.

Hiking Trails of the Ocala National Forest

The Ocala National Forest is located in north-central Florida and is a place of contrasts. On one hand, the vegetation of its rolling hills constitutes the largest reforest maining stretch of the sand pine scrub that once covered much of the central part of the state. Sand pine scrub is a forest type that grows on fast-draining sandy soils. Sand pines are often surrounded by scrub oaks and other plants that tolerate the dry conditions. Lands like this are easily developed and have all but disappeared in Florida, making this large conserved area of it that much more valuable. Attendant wildlife species such as the scrub jay are dependent upon this kind of habitat.

On the other hand, this national forest has numerous natural lakes and springs. The shallow lakes scattered throughout the forest are watery oases in the sand pines. Grassy prairies often surround the lakes, offering far-reaching views. The springs of the Ocala are world famous. Juniper Springs, Alexander Springs, and others are clear, alluring waters that create a semitropical setting. Recreation areas offering swimming, nature walks, canoeing, and camping have sprung up around these springs.

For hikers, the Ocala features a 60-mile unbroken segment of the Florida Trail, running from Clearwater Lake in the south to Rodman Reservoir in the north. This section passes many springs and more lakes and traverses the unique sand pine scrub. It offers opportunities from short there-and-back day hikes to multinight backpacking trips. This portion of the FT, which used to be known as the Ocala Trail, is one of the most popular sections of the entire Florida Trail system. An added hiking bonus is the walk through the Juniper Prairie Wilderness, which captures the Ocala at its most primitive.

There are other paths that traverse this forest, including a lengthy new portion of the Florida Trail headed southwest to connect with the Cross Florida Greenway. Other examples are the St. Francis Interpretive Trail, which wanders the lush bottomland of the St. Francis Dead River, a side channel off the upper St. Johns River. Near Lake Eaton a path gets to the bottom of why there are so many limestone sinkholes here. Other nature trails in the Ocala offer more information about the whys and wherefores of the woods.

Florida Trail, Clearwater Lake to State Road 19

Begin: Clearwater Lake
End: State Road 19
Distance: 13.5 miles
Trail Difficulty: Moderate
Highlights: Numerous forest environments, spring-fed creek, ponds, and prairies
Hazards: Potentially confusing jeep trail crossings
Trail Connections: Florida Trail, State Road 19 to Juniper Springs; Alexander Springs Spur Trail
Season: Late fall–spring
Maps: Florida Trail Ocala South, Ocala National Forest map
Trailhead: From the Seminole Ranger Station in Umatilla, drive north on SR 19 for 1.5 miles to CR 42. Turn right on CR 42, and head east for 6.3 miles to Clearwater Lake Recreation Area. The trailhead starts on the right 50 yards after the left turn to Clearwater Lake.

The Florida Trail had its beginnings here in the Ocala in 1966. At first it was called the Ocala Trail. Some still call the Ocala portion of the Florida Trail by its old name. No matter the name, this section of trail starts out a little civilized, then passes some prairie and pond environments. Later it crosses one of the Ocala's few surface streams, then goes through rolling longleaf pine land to enter the classic sand pine scrub for which the national forest is known.

The actual beginning of the Florida Trail in the Ocala National Forest starts a quarter mile east of the entrance to Clearwater Lake Recreation Area on County Road 42. But parking there is less than ideal. So for purposes of practicality in this guidebook, the description starts at the Clearwater Lake parking area.

Start your hike on the spur trail leaving east from the parking area. Enter a longleaf pine forest, descend into a flat, and climb a bit through oak and sand pine to intersect the Florida Trail at 0.3 mile. The Florida Trail has come 0.3 mile south of this junction from CR 42.

Turn left and head north on the orange-blazed FT. Cross the Paisley Woods Bicycle Trail a couple of times, as well as a few obscure jeep and ATV trails, but the course of the FT is rarely in doubt. Houses are visible on private land to your right.

At mile 1.9 cross Paisley Road, Forest Road 538, then descend and roll through open longleaf pine and scrub oak woods. Needle-covered sand forms the footbed. Watch for trailside cacti. At mile 3.8, pass a large prairie encircling Duck Pond. Leave the north end of the prairie at mile 4.3 and traverse a nearly pure stand of turkey oaks that gives way to open flatwoods.

At mile 4.8, pass under a major power line. Stay right and look for an orange blaze entering a palmetto thicket. The trail passes through longleaf pine woods until descending to a moister area and Glenn Branch at mile 5.3. This creek has cool clear water and allows moisture-loving trees such as maple to thrive. There are campsites in the area. Look uphill for level spots.

Span Glenn Branch on a footbridge and emerge into pine flatwoods featuring pond pine as well as slash and longleaf pine. At mile 5.4, a boardwalk bisects the jungle of palm-maple-oak swamp. Encounter more boardwalks before coming out on FR 539 at mile 6.6.

Enter mixed pine flatwoods across the road and turn northwest. Cross a small prairie to your left at mile 6.8. Soon after this the forest transitions to sand pine and its attendant scrub oak understory. Cross FR 538A at mile 8.4. As the trail nears Alexander Springs, the woods to your right drop off sharply toward the spring run. At mile 9.7, take a long boardwalk over a sporadically wet area. Come to the junction with the Alexander Springs Spur Trail at mile 10.1.

At Alexander Springs, there is potable water available. The Alexander Springs Spur Trail leads right to merge with the Paisley Woods Bicycle Trail and come out on CR 445. Cross the paved road and enter the recreation area at 0.5 mile for camping, swimming, canoeing, and parking.

The Florida Trail, however, continues forward, soon to cross FR 538. Leave the rich and varied unburned woods of the recreation area to enter rolling longleaf and turkey oak woods with a more recent burning history. At mile 11.0, cross paved CR 445. By mile 11.7, the forest has transitioned to mature sand pine scrub. A younger sand pine scrub is on trail right, then on both sides of the trail. This adds up to few shade-bearing mature sand pines overhead. The forest thickens, though, before emerging onto State Road 19 at mile 13.5. Ahead, the Florida Trail continues north for 13.8 miles to Juniper Springs.

Florida Trail, State Road 19 to Juniper Springs

Begin: State Road 19
End: Juniper Springs Recreation Area
Distance: 13.8 miles
Trail Difficulty: Moderate
Highlights: Big prairies and lakes, rolling hills, isolation
Hazards: None
Trail Connections: Florida Trail, Clearwater Lake to State Road 19; Florida Trail, Juniper Springs to Hopkins Prairie
Season: Late fall–spring
Maps: Florida Trail Ocala South, Ocala National Forest map
Trailhead: From the Seminole Ranger Station in Umatilla, drive north on SR 19 for 9.1 miles to the Florida Trail parking area on your left off SR 19.

This section of the Florida Trail passes through some scenic and remote territory of the Ocala National Forest. The route alternates between the open natural lakes and rolling sand hills of the state's Central Ridge. The lake country features far-reaching views and cool waters. The sand pine scrub forests cover high hills offering vertical variation little seen in Florida. Some of the most remote territory on this hike borders a naval bombing range, so airplane noise is a possibility, but the range means that the surrounding wild country is much more extensive than just the national forest.

Start your hike by leaving SR 19 and following the orange blazes north. You are in a mature forest, but there is a sun- whipped cut-over area just to your left. Watch for the proliferation of holly in the forest understory. This shrubby tree grows bright red berries seen in the cooler months.

Pass a small sink on your left at 0.4 mile. Cross CR 9277, Railroad Grade Road, at 0.9 mile. Come to your first wet prairie ringed in live oak, called Summit Pond. Live oak and longleaf pines often are found in the moister, more fertile soils. Keep north as the woods briefly revert back to sand pine scrub before coming to an attractive and sizable pond at mile 1.5. There are potential campsites around this quiet locale.

Swing around the north end of the pond and climb into sand pine hills again. The trees here have reached maturity and are beginning to fall. Sand pines are a short-lived species—after about fifty to seventy years they begin to succumb to old age and disease. These trees rarely see a century.

At mile 1.9, reach the blue-blazed Buck Lake Loop Trail. This trail leads around the east side of Buck Lake past a forest service campground. The Florida Trail leads left around the west side of Buck Lake. Stay left with the orange blazes. At first, the trail stays far from Buck Lake, although you gain glimpses of the water. At mile 2.4, come to the north end of the Buck Lake Loop Trail. The loop trail leads right 0.3 mile to a pump well for water access.

Stay forward on the Florida Trail, soon crossing FR 562-2. Undulate west through a mature sand pine forest. At mile 2.8 a side trail leads right to a quiet pond, Yearling Pond. Past the pond the trail skirts some cut-over areas with minimal shade. Swing around a small pond to your left before coming to the blue- blazed side trail to Farles Prairie Campground at mile 4.1. This side trail leads right a short distance to pump well water.

Continue forward and shortly cross FR 595E. The forest reverts to mixed pine before coming to FR 595 at mile 4.4. Cross the sandy road and soon come to a second blue-blazed side trail to Farles Prairie Campground. This side trail leads right 0.2 mile to water. Beyond the side trail numerous ponds and prairies dot the thick forest.

Florida is known as the Sunshine State, but it is also a very watery place. There are around 7,800 lakes in the state, most of them small. The nearest concentration of natural lakes is far north in Wisconsin, which has over 5,000 lakes. Most Florida lakes have been formed by dissolution of the limestone rock that underlies much of the state. Underwater caverns form in the limestone. Then the naturally acidic rain dissolves the limestone, causing the caverns to collapse, and lakes are formed.

Come alongside particularly large prairies to your left and right. This is greater Farles Prairie, a great place to camp; in my numerous ramblings here I have never heard bombing in the range to the west. Live oaks and longleaf pine thrive alongside the lakes here. At mile 6.2, pass through a sand pine woodland and emerge onto more large prairies in a half mile. These prairies, collectively known as Ocala Pond, are very shallow, not holding much water, and have pines growing sporadically among them. The hurricanes of the new millennium have raised the water levels, though. There are good vistas here.

At mile 7.8, turn away from the shallow prairies, keeping north and rolling through sand pine wood to intersect FR 599 at mile 8.4. Stay in sand pine and roller-coaster through some of the Ocala's most exceptional sand pine hills. Drop to a small prairie on your right at mile 11.0, and reenter sand pine woods. The trail enters one final prairie region at mile 11.8. The moister, lower area transitions to live oaks, maples, and palms, culminating in a boardwalk crossing a wet area at mile 12.3. Leave the wet area just before coming to paved SR 40 at mile 12.6.

Cross SR 40 and head north into the south end of the Juniper Prairie Wilderness. From here the trail begins a long loop around Juniper Run. The orange-blazed path turns west, roughly paralleling SR 40 through a mixed pine forest with an oak and palmetto understory. Leave the wilderness at 13.2 miles. The woods here were devastated by Hurricanes Jeanne and Francis in 2004, so the forest service executed a timber cutting. The hills are open between here and the paved entrance road to the Juniper Springs Recreation Area campground at 13.8 miles, ending this section of the Florida Trail. From here it is 10.9 miles north to Hopkins Prairie on the Florida Trail.

Florida Trail, Juniper Springs to Hopkins Prairie

Begin: Juniper Springs Recreation Area
End: Hopkins Prairie
Distance: 10.9 miles
Trail Difficulty: Moderate to difficult
Highlights: Juniper Prairie Wilderness, vistas, Hidden Pond
Hazards: Sun exposure, possibly confusing trail turns
Trail Connections: Florida Trail, State Road 19 to Juniper Springs; Florida Trail, Hopkins Prairie to Salt Springs Island; The Yearling Trail
Season: Late fall–spring
Maps: Florida Trail Ocala South, Ocala National Forest map
Trailhead: From Ocala, drive east on SR 40 for 28 miles to Juniper Springs Recreation Area, on your left. The Florida Trail starts on the entrance road to the recreation area. Hikers can choose to park an auto inside the recreation area for a fee.

This section of the Florida Trail passes through the rugged Juniper Prairie Wilderness, a land of sand pine scrub forest, ponds, and prairies. The FT here receives less maintenance than on some segments, so hikers step over logs and under low-lying oak limbs. Vegetation grows tightly along the path. Most old jeep roads are growing over, and hurricanes have felled trees over abandoned tracks; there are some confusing points—stay with the orange blazes.

The trail also passes through low-lying pine scrub, where the sun blazes down from above. Bears roam along Whiskey Creek, Pat's Island reveals its past, and the cool waters of Hidden Pond await your arrival. The tops of hills and the open prairies allow for far-reaching views. Once past Juniper Prairie, the FT passes through a pleasant woodland to end at Hopkins Prairie, where there are more good vistas and a campground.

Start your hike by leaving west from the recreation area access road on the Florida Trail. This open area was timbered following the forest devastation from Hurricanes Jeanne and Francis. At mile 0.4 enter low burned-over oak scrub with an occasional tall sand pine. This section is exposed, but the exposure allows vistas of the hilly terrain. A young forest like this is essential for the perpetuation of species such as the scrub jay and gopher tortoise, which are rapidly losing habitat.

The scrub jay is an interesting inhabitant of the Ocala. It is a fire-dependent bird that requires a low shrub layer with no canopy. Scrub jays feed on insects, but they also eat acorns in the fall. When a forest ages and a sand pine canopy rises, scrub jays leave the area. With occasional fires, certain areas of the forest stay young and low, making for good scrub jay habitat.

Turn north and briefly enter a mature sand pine forest before turning back east. You are circling around Juniper Springs. At mile 1.2 enter the Juniper Prairie Wilderness. The trail narrows as it passes through sand pine scrub woods in many stages of succession. Hike through an open pine flatwoods environment at mile 2.2, to view the first of many prairies and ponds.

Pass some conspicuous palms at mile 3.0 and step over a prairie outflow, Whispering Creek, on piled logs. Emerge into low sand pine scrub before descending to Whiskey Creek. Step over this perennial stream on a plank footbridge at mile 3.7. The woods are thicker here. There are campsites uphill on the creek's north side. There is much bear sign as well.

Keep north and emerge into low pine scrub with many dead snags rising from its flanks. Top out on a hill—there are good views in all directions. Swing around a small sink to your left before coming to Hidden Pond at mile 4.9. This is a good swimming hole. There is a heavily used camping site in the oaks on the far side of the pond. The Florida Trail, however, stays to the right of the pond and reenters young scrub.

Climb away from Hidden Pond and keep north to gain some shade from a patchwork forest at mile 5.1. The trail briefly merges with and then crosses an old jeep road. Stay with the large prairie to your left. The trail turns away from the large prairie at mile 5.5 and primarily stays in an oak forest as it zigzags between scattered ponds and small prairies.

Leave the primary prairie area at mile 6.3, and undulate through sand pine woodland that was devastated by storms in 2004. Downed trees border the trail. Come to one more small prairie area at mile 7.0. Climb up a hill to a signed trail junction at mile 7.7. Here a spur trail leads right for 0.6 mile to Pat's Island and the Long Cemetery. From the cemetery, turn left on the spur trail and head 0.3 mile to a large dry sinkhole.

Figure 11. Looking out over a pond in Juniper Prairie Wilderness. Photo by Johnny Molloy

This cemetery and nearby sinkhole can also be accessed via The Yearling Trail.

The Florida Trail continues forward from the signed junction, entering longleaf pine woods before leaving the Juniper Prairie Wilderness and coming to FR 10 at mile 8.1. There is a trailhead parking area just to the east of the road crossing. Cross the forest road and enter an oak and sand pine forest, parts of which were timbered in the mid-2000s. The trail meanders north to pass a sink just before emerging onto FR 86 at mile 9.0.

Cross FR 86 and enter the edge of the Hopkins Prairie Recreation Area. Pass to the right of a chilly swimming hole, to enter oak woodland draped in Spanish moss. There are views to your left of Hopkins Prairie, one of the most extensive prairies in the Ocala.

At mile 9.6, cross the Hopkins Prairie campground access road, FR 86F. Stay with the orange blazes as the path winds among jeep trails behind the campground. Emerge onto Hopkins Prairie at mile 10.1. The Florida Trail turns abruptly to the right. To your left is Hopkins Prairie campground, which has pump well water, toilets, campsites, and hiker parking. From here it is 8.3 miles north to Salt Springs Island on the Florida Trail.

Florida Trail, Hopkins Prairie
to Salt Springs Island

Begin: Hopkins Prairie Campground
End: Forest Road 88 near Salt Springs
Distance: 8.6 miles
Trail Difficulty: Moderate
Highlights: Hopkins Prairie, longleaf-wiregrass ecosystem
Hazards: Potentially confusing jeep trail intersections, loose sand
Trail Connections: Salt Springs Spur Trail; Florida Trail, Juniper Springs to Hopkins Prairie; Florida Trail, Salt Springs Island to Lake Delancy
Season: Late fall–spring
Maps: Florida Trail Ocala North, Ocala National Forest map
Trailhead: From Ocala, head east on SR 40 for 12 miles to Marion County Road 314. Turn left on CR 314 and follow it 18 miles to SR 19. Turn right on SR 19 and follow it for 7.8 miles to FR 86. Turn right on FR 86 and follow it for 2.4 miles to FR 86F. Turn right on FR 86F and follow it for 0.7 mile to Hopkins Prairie Campground. The Florida Trail starts at the end of the right campground spur road.

For more than four miles this portion of the Florida Trail skirts the edge of Hopkins Prairie, the largest prairie in the Ocala, offering numerous vistas for the hiker. It then leaves the large wetland for a region of smaller prairies to enter a longleaf-wiregrass woodland, a habitat once prevalent across Florida and the Gulf states. This rolling land of towering longleaf pines and knee-high wiregrass offers vistas of its own. It is a lightly used section of the FT that deserves more recognition for its beauty.

Leave the right spur road of Hopkins Prairie Campground and hike just a few yards on a blue-blazed trail to intersect the Florida Trail. Stay left, heading north along the right edge of Hopkins Prairie on an old jeep road. The first of numerous prairie vistas lies on your left through the pines that border the pond-pocked wetland.

Another much smaller broken prairie comes into view off to your right. The trail sometimes bisects the winding Hopkins Prairie border through shady oak hammocks as it heads northwest. In other areas there is no canopy overhead, and hikers are exposed to the elements above and loose sand below. More views reveal the north end of the prairie.

At mile 2.9 the trail makes a nearly 180-degree turn back to the southeast around an oak hammock. At mile 3.9, a side trail leads uphill and to the right, to meet Forest Road 90. The Florida Trail continues to parallel the prairie perimeter.

At mile 4.3 make a sharp right turn into a low oak thicket, leaving Hopkins Prairie. The Florida Trail reaches FR 65 at mile 4.5. Cross the sandy road and enter a sand pine scrub forest with a thick understory. Next, cross FR 90 at mile 4.8 and make a noticeable descent. Stay in a rolling sand pine scrub woodland.

At mile 5.4 the trail winds through numerous small prairies on a pine-oak strand of high ground. Come to a trail junction and wooden resting bench at mile 6.0. The Salt Springs Spur Trail leads 3.1 miles to the marina road at the Salt Springs Recreation Area. The hamlet of Salt Springs is near the recreation area, where supplies are available for long distance hikers.

Keep northwesterly on the Florida Trail through a young scrub woodland. Turkey oaks become more abundant. Cross FR 51, and soon come to FR 50 at mile 6.8. On the far side of this road the longleaf-wiregrass ecosystem begins. This pine and grass landscape used to cover over three million acres in the Southeast.

Fire is a necessary and critical component of this forest. Fire suppression, along with development, have played roles in its demise. This attractive forest has good vistas in its own right, especially where the terrain begins to undulate. Scattered oak hammocks increase as you near FR 88. This is the east edge of Salt Springs Island. Come to paved FR 88 at mile 8.6. From here it is 11.4 miles to Lake Delancy Campground.

Florida Trail, Salt Springs Island to Lake Delancy

Begin: Salt Springs Island
End: Delancy West Campground
Distance: 11.4 miles
Trail Difficulty: Moderate
Highlights: Salt Springs Island, Kerr Island
Hazards: Occasional indistinguishable trailbed
Trail Connections: Florida Trail, Hopkins Prairie to Salt Springs Island; Florida Trail, Lake Delancy to Rodman Dam; Florida Trail Western Corridor
Season: Late fall–spring
Maps: Florida Trail Ocala North, Ocala National Forest map
Trailhead: From Ocala, head east on SR 40 for 12 miles to CR 314. Turn left on CR 314 and follow it 15.4 miles to paved FR 88. Turn right on FR 88 and follow it for 0.4 mile to the Florida Trail. There is parking on the left side of the road, just before the Florida Trail crosses FR 88.

This section of the Florida Trail passes over two "islands" in the Ocala, Kerr Island and Salt Springs Island. These islands are not surrounded by water in the traditional definition of the word but are islands of more fertile soil, supporting rich stands of longleaf and slash pine, surrounded by poorer soils that support the sand pine scrub environment so prevalent in the Ocala. This section of the Florida Trail is less used than in other Ocala locations and thus offers more opportunities for solitude, even though the path does cross some roads.

Leave FR 88 and head northwest on the orange-blazed Florida Trail. You are on the eastern end of Salt Springs Island. Enter a longleaf pine forest with a mixed understory of grass and very young oak scrub. Come to and cross paved CR 314 at 0.4 mile. Continue in a longleaf and turkey oak forest, with scattered small oak hammocks. Cross FR 19 at mile 1.4.

Beyond here the trailbed becomes less evident. Watch for the orange blazes painted on trees while keeping northwesterly. Cross sandy and small FR 50 at mile 1.7. This road is the northwest border of Salt Springs

Figure 12. Longleaf-wiregrass forest is an important part of the Ocala National Forest ecosystem. Photo by Johnny Molloy

Island. Past here, the forest reverts to sand pine scrub. Enter mature sand pine scrub at 0.2 mile. This especially attractive neck of the woods has a thick understory.

The trail then enters a section of the forest that alternates between older sand pines and younger low scrub. After an extended section of low scrub, come to high pine woods and FR 63 at mile 3.3. This is the south end of Kerr Island. Keep north into a forest of longleaf pine and turkey oak with a grass and shrub understory. The trailbed here is again less evident, but the orange blazes will keep you on the right path.

Cross FR 63 again at mile 3.9. The forest transitions back to sand pine scrub on the far side of FR 63. Reenter Kerr Island at mile 4.3 after crossing FR 63 a third time. At mile 4.6, the Western Corridor of the Florida Trail comes in from the left, after having split with the Eastern Corridor south of Orlando. Those who hike the Florida Trail have two options to get around Orlando, the Eastern Corridor or the Western Corridor.

Make one more forest road crossing before reaching the blue-blazed spur trail at 5.0 miles to the 88 Store, a combination convenience store and bar with limited supplies and showers. The spur trail travels 0.4 mile through mostly planted pines before climbing a hill to the store. Camping is possible on forest land along the spur trail, but hikers need to get water from the store.

The Florida Trail passes through some pine plantations then a stumpy former firewood-cutting area before reaching CR 316 at mile 5.7.

Walk into an area of sand pine scrub that is fairly young and does not provide much canopy. The sandy trailbed can be loose. Cross FR 88-4 at mile 6.3. The low scrub remains on the far side of FR 88. The rolling nature of the landscape is evident over the woods. Swing past Prairie Pond on your left at mile 6.9, before passing rough FR 88C. Intersect the first of two short blue-blazed side trails to Grassy Pond Campground at mile 7.1. This open campground is less than desirable, but it has the only water for miles. The pump well once located here has been taken out, so you must get water from the pond.

The FT makes a sharp right at a T-junction just past the campground. Continue north in low pine scrub, heavy on sand live oak. The canopy resumes at mile 7.7. There is much deer moss on the forest floor. Small oak hammocks are scattered over the rolling hills. Pass a private inholding on trail left, then swing into an attractive longleaf-wiregrass woodland. The forest becomes mixed, with both longleaf and sand pine scrub forest species represented. A real sense of remoteness falls over the land here.

Oaks increase as you near Lake Delancy. There are some really large high pines in the woods here, too. At mile 10.7, drop down and pass by a dry sink on your left. Soon cross FR 56. Keep forward, crossing FR 85A. The campground lies off to your right. Intersect FR 75-2 at mile 11.4. The entrance to Delancy West Campground is just off to your right. Blue blazes lead along FR 75-2 to the pump well at nearby Delancy East Campground. From here it is 7.3 miles north on the Florida Trail to Rodman Dam.

Florida Trail, Lake Delancy to Rodman Dam

Begin: West Delancy Campground
End: Rodman Dam
Distance: 7.3 miles
Trail Difficulty: Moderate
Highlights: Riverside Island, Penner Ponds, Rodman Reservoir
Hazards: None
Trail Connections: Florida Trail, Salt Springs Island to Lake Delancy; Penner Ponds Spur Trail
Season: Late fall–spring
Maps: Florida Trail Ocala North, Ocala National Forest map
Trailhead: From Ocala, drive east on SR 40 for 12 miles to CR 314. Turn left on CR 314 and follow it 18 miles to SR 19. Turn left on SR 19 and follow it north 5.4 miles to FR 75. Turn left on FR 75 and follow it 3.3 miles to Delancy West Campground. The Florida Trail starts just past the entrance to Delancy West Campground.

This is the most northerly segment of the Florida Trail through the Ocala National Forest. It rolls over Riverside Island, with attractive pine stands, then passes Penner Ponds, the last prairie-pond complex in the forest. Finally, the path comes to Rodman Reservoir, an impoundment that is part of the now defunct Cross Florida Barge Canal project. Nonetheless, the lakeside scenery is attractive and the land remote before you leave the national forest and end up on the far side of Rodman Dam.

Start your hike by heading north from Delancy West Campground and into a longleaf forest. Wiregrass, turkey oaks, and dense stands of young live oaks cover the landscape. The dense stands of oaks are sometimes referred to as oak domes, for the continuous leaf canopy is lower at the edges and higher in the center. At mile 1.3, the trail cuts through the heart of a shady oak dome.

Beyond this oak dome, longleaf pines begin to dominate the forest. Ferns, flowers, grass, and occasional saw palmetto rise from the open woodland floor. At mile 1.8, descend alongside a sink to your left. The

Figure 13. The shores of the Rodman Reservoir are often lined with driftwood. Photo by Johnny Molloy

sink has an open grassy bottom surrounded by large live oaks. It exhibits a lusher look than the surrounding pine forest.

At mile 2.0, cross FR 88-4. Reenter the pine forest of Riverside Island. Notice all the young longleaf pines. They have a spindly main stem coming up from the ground and are topped with a single bulblike expanse of needles emerging from the top of the plant. These pines are using all their energy to grow their trunks tall enough to be able to withstand a low-intensity lightning-caused ground fire, like those that often swept through such forests before fire suppression. Once they are tall enough, the longleaf pines begin to branch out and gain height.

The longleaf-wiregrass forest loses dominance as you head north. Turkey oaks and scrub oaks become more prevalent. Cross FR 31 at mile 3.7. Keep rolling over the land and drop down to a sink on your right. Sand pines and longleaf blend past the sink.

Cross FR 31A at mile 4.5, then come to another sandy road with a power line. Leave the pines behind and walk in an oak woodland of varying ages before coming out on FR 77-1. Just across the road a blue-blazed spur trail leads left to and around Penner Ponds. This is the most northerly pond-prairie complex in the Ocala that the FT bypasses. Beyond this side trail, which was the old route of the Florida Trail, the path has been rerouted and the trailbed is sometimes not evident.

Wind through a mixed forest with intense thickets of sand pine before crossing rough FR 77A. Pass a tiny pond on your left and come to the north end of the side trail to Penner Ponds at mile 5.7. Turn sharply right to enter mature sand pine woods. This area slowly transitions to a live oak forest draped in Spanish moss before coming to the shores of Lake Ocklawaha. Turn right again in this beautiful area with camping potential, cruising eastward along the shores of the impoundment. Stay alongside the beach-lined shore of Rodman Reservoir. Emerge into an open area at mile 6.7, passing a trail kiosk on your right. Rodman Dam lies to your left. Turn left and walk the dam road 0.7 mile to the far side of the dam. Steps lead to a parking area just below the dam, by a dock and the dam spillway.

The directions for this parking area on the north end of the Florida Trail are as follows: From Ocala, drive west on SR 40 for 12 miles to CR 314. Turn left on CR 314 and follow it 18 miles to SR 19. Turn left on SR 19 and follow it north for 11.7 miles to CR 310 (Kirkpatrick Road) and Kirkpatrick Recreation Area. Turn left on CR 310 and follow it 3.2 miles to the dam. The parking area is the north side below the dam. There is also parking at Rodman Dam Campground, which you pass on the way to the dam.

Florida Trail, Western Connector North, Eaton Creek to Eastern Corridor Junction

Begin: Eaton Creek Trailhead
End: Eastern Corridor Junction
Distance: 10.9 miles
Trail Difficulty: Moderate
Highlights: Moss-lined footpath through scrub forest
Hazards: Heat, soft sand, insects
Trail Connections: Florida Trail, Western Connector South; Florida Trail, Salt Springs Island to Lake Delancy
Season: Fall–spring
Maps: Florida Trail, Cross Florida Greenway East
Trailhead: From the intersection of SR 40 and CR 314 at Nuby's Corner, drive north on CR 314 for 9 miles to NE 172nd Ave, just north of CR 314A. There is a sign for an environmental education camp. Turn right. The trailhead is 1 mile up the road on the right.

Under construction to link the main Florida Trail through the Ocala National Forest and the Florida Trail on the Cross Florida Greenway, the new Florida Trail Western Connector traverses a variety of habitats along the western fringe of the Big Scrub. From the Eaton Creek Trailhead north, the trail is high and dry and showcases the entire life cycle of the sand pine scrub ecosystem. This is a linear hike, so you may want to work out a shuttle or a second car placed at the 88 Store along FR 88 near Lake Kerr. Be sure to ask permission before leaving a car there. This portion of the trail can be enjoyed as a long day hike or a two-day backpacking trip.

Start your hike at the Eaton Creek Trailhead kiosk. Follow the blue blazes adjoining the power line for almost 0.1 mile to a T-junction with the orange-blazed Florida Trail. Turn left to walk along a well-defined corridor edged by saw palmetto. A broad spot in the trail would make a good place for camping. The trail turns left here, passing under the power line and crossing Northeast 172nd Avenue. It becomes more of a forest road than a footpath, a long straight corridor that pops out into a recently logged area with only small stands of forest to provide shade. You reach an intersection of sand roads at 0.7 mile. Continue straight. Look for bear tracks in the sand. At 1.4 miles the trail follows a firebreak around shady woods next to a bayhead and then turns off the firebreak to the left. Keep alert for the turn, which leads you down a narrow, shady corridor under tall sand pines.

After 2 miles, you cross CR 314 at a power line. Watch for high-speed traffic. Continue into the forest at the Florida Trail sign. The LAM Equestrian Trail parallels the Florida Trail under the power line. There is a nice open grassy spot for tenting but no nearby water source. Walk under the power line and enjoy the shade of a lush hardwood forest surrounding Mud Lake. The trail turns right, but if you need to filter water, follow an old wagon road down to the lake by going straight ahead.

As the trail climbs back into the sand pine forest, it crosses a jeep trail that leads downhill to a stream that serves as a reliable water source. Follow a fence around private property, cross the driveway, and look for a T-intersection at a junction of jeep roads. The blaze is on a post. At a Y-intersection at 3.5 miles, keep left. You pass an open, dry spot for camping. The Ocklawaha River is off to the left through a screen of floodplain forest and tall longleaf pines and magnolias. At 4 miles, a stand of prairie grass fills a small clearing. Soon after, the trail rises back up into the sand pine scrub, making a sharp left uphill into prime scrub jay habitat.

Following the orange blazes, you make numerous sharp turns. As you walk through a tall stand of sand pines, they creak like bamboo poles rubbing together. Cross FR 67, a major unpaved road, at 5.1 miles. The trail heads down a moss-lined corridor, a beauty spot under the pines, showcasing the best of the Big Scrub. Notice how you pass through different heights and ages of sand pine forest. That's because this is a fire-based ecosystem, requiring fire for regeneration. All pines within any particular area will be the same age.

Cross FR 67 again at 5.6 miles and start a gradual uphill stretch. The trail passes under another power line. At 6 miles there are logs along the trail that provide a good place to take a break. Another power line is overhead before you cross FR 67 for the third and final time. Continue on a pleasant meander through medium-sized sand pines. You may hear the sound of thunder in the distance—Air Force bombing practice at the bombing range to the east. Drop down around a depression and circle a small sink. The habitat becomes more desertlike, with whiter sand and tiny trees, and then denser, with soft pine duff underfoot. After 8 miles you cross FR 97 and continue through the scrub forest. A jeep path crosses and then curves past on the right. The understory under the tall trees is open and has clusters of saw palmetto and spongy deer moss. The tall pines clatter and warble.

The trail makes a sharp left to follow the edge between an older pine forest and a younger one. Another sharp left leads you into a dense stand of small trees. Cross a jeep road before you reach the trail junction at 10.1 miles with the Florida Trail Eastern Corridor on Salt Springs Island. To reach the nearest trailhead, turn left. The habitat transitions to sand hills with turkey oaks beneath tall longleaf pines. Follow the undulating hills another 0.4 mile north to the "88 Store" sign and water symbol. Follow the blue blaze from this trail junction another 0.4 mile through pine plantations to the 88 Store, a popular watering hole, barbecue, and hiker-friendly destination along FR 88 near Lake Kerr. When you reach the store, you've hiked 10.9 miles. For a small fee they offer tent camping with showers, restrooms, and self-service laundry behind the store. Alternatively, you can walk 1 mile north from the trail junction to reach CR 316, where hikers are permitted to leave their cars at the Hunt Check Station within sight of the trail crossing.

Florida Trail, Western Connector South, Eaton Creek to 145th Ave

Begin: Eaton Creek Trailhead
End: NE 145th Ave
Distance: 5.6 miles
Trail Difficulty: Difficult
Highlights: Eaton Creek, fern forests, cypress boardwalk
Hazards: Tall vegetation, deep mud holes, insects, losing the trail
Trail Connections: Florida Trail Western Connector North
Season: Fall–spring
Maps: Florida Trail, Cross Florida Greenway East
Trailhead: From the intersection of SR 40 and CR 314 at Nuby's Corner, drive north on CR 314 for 9 miles to NE 172nd Ave, just north of CR 314A. There is a sign for an environmental education camp. Turn right. The trailhead is 1 mile up the road on the right.

Under construction to link the main Florida Trail through the Ocala National Forest and the Florida Trail on the Cross Florida Greenway, the new Florida Trail Western Connector traverses a variety of habitats along the western fringe of the Big Scrub. From the Eaton Creek Trailhead south, the trail enters a tangled jungle of rampant growth along tiny streams and tributaries flowing into the Ocklawaha River. It also passes through many pine plantations that are reverting back to wild wet flatwoods. While the intent is to complete this trail to connect to the Cross Florida Greenway, there are swamps with quicksandlike mud to be dealt with along some of the tributaries south of NE 145th Ave. Please do not proceed south from that point unless the trail is explicitly posted as open.

Start your hike at the Eaton Creek Trailhead kiosk. Follow the blue blazes adjoining the power line for almost 0.1 mile to a T-junction with the Florida Trail. Turn right and follow the orange blazes into a lush floodplain forest. A boardwalk leads you to the Eaton Creek Bridge, a scenic spot, where tannic water sluices past islands in this broad creek that drains Lake Eaton. Tall hickory trees and cabbage palms rise from the forest floor. Cross the bridge and turn left. The pines are simply enormous here.

At a junction with a forest road, turn right. You pass an unusual natural landmark: a hickory tree with four branching trunks coming out of a very thick base. At a clearing, the trail makes a sharp right. A large pond sits off to the left at 0.4 mile, big enough to be a water source. Make sure you look for the next blaze at the junction of forest roads. The trail twists and winds through scrub forest and reaches a jeep road. At 1 mile, you see a small faux rock garden of busted-up concrete surrounded by scrub plants. Turn sharply right and follow the trail over undulating plow lines amid a pine plantation.

After 1.3 miles, the trail emerges onto CR 314A. Cross the road and look for the trail entrance offset over to your right. It enters mesic flatwoods on a well-defined path between the saw palmettos. The trail then enters a bayhead swamp with tall ferns. Some of the ferns may be over your head. Beware of where you step, as there are deep mud holes in a few spots. You reach a welcome boardwalk and follow it into the depths of the bayhead swamp to pass by an island of large slash pines, each of which shows evidence of turpentine tapping. Bog bridges lead you into another area where ferns grow to enormous proportions. The trail becomes hummocky as it crosses over old plow lines.

After 1.6 miles, you reach a forest road. Turn left. The blazes lead to a set of bog bridges that skirt the edge of a flowing stream. The bridges provide a nice place to enjoy this tropical setting. The habitat transitions to old scrub pine forest with a dense understory, and the trail emerges onto an ecotone between pine flatwoods and scrub. It crosses a jeep trail at 2.1 miles, entering wet flatwoods and a pine plantation. Bog bridges guide you through another bayhead swamp. The trail drops down into a hummocky area with bog bridges over the low spots before it reaches the NE 52nd Place road crossing at 2.4 miles.

From NE 52nd Place the trail leads you south through a young pine plantation, paralleling the road. A wall of cypress to your left indicates a creek. This area went through a prescribed burn in spring 2006. The blazes and footpath may be indistinct. The trail veers around a bayhead at 2.9 miles and then takes off to the left through a pine plantation. After 3.2 miles, you leave the younger industrial-style pine plantation for a habitat with taller, older pines and normal understory plants. You cross a firebreak and turn left to start the cypress boardwalk. This series of

Figure 14. Hikers celebrating National Trails Day leave the Eaton Creek Bridge on the Florida Trail's Western Connector. Photo by Sandra Friend

low-impact bridges connects islands in the creek's floodplain, with lots of cinnamon fern growing between them. The third bridge runs more than a quarter mile through a shady glade beneath cypresses and pines. Beware the monstrous poison ivy vines dangling just overhead.

You leave the scenic boardwalk at 3.5 miles and a enter forest of taller pines. Turn left on the firebreak and reach a Y-junction of forest roads at 3.8 miles. The footpath veers off to the left to parallel the forest road. Pass a marsh in a large depression on the left, and keep to the left at the forest road junction. To the left is natural forest, to the right, pine plantation. Watch for where the trail veers off the road to the left and heads into the forest around mile 4.0. Follow the path into the pines; a cypress-lined creek is off in the distance to your left. The trail drops down through a cool spot in a bayhead swamp at 4.5 miles and enters a serious stand of saw palmetto under the tall pines. Be alert for mud holes in the road crossing.

After 4.6 miles the footpath vanishes beneath immense ferns growing out of tall hummocks, and you must rely entirely on the blazes to guide you. Spot the next one before walking in any direction, or you may end up walking in circles amid the giant ferns. Some of the low spots between the hummocks have mud holes or deep pine duff into which it is easy to sink a shoe. Once you are through the fern forest, the trail reaches the edge of the denser pine forest and follows it. Terrestrial orchids rise from the perpetually damp ground. The trail leads between more giant ferns under the tall pines and past ancient saw palmetto lifting their trunks well off the ground. The low spots between the ferns get wetter and more difficult to traverse. You can hear road noise in the distance. The trail reaches a long boardwalk over a perpetually damp sphagnum moss bog at 5.4 miles. A short stretch of footpath leads to a final boardwalk over a roadside marsh, depositing you at the NE 145th Ave trail crossing after 5.6 rugged miles.

If your intent is to backpack through to the Florida Trail along the Cross Florida Greenway, you must roadwalk from here to the Marshall Swamp Trailhead west of the Ocklawaha River unless the trail is explicitly signposted as open. To do so, turn right and cross the highway bridge over Hulls Creek. Walk west along Northeast 145th Avenue, which turns into NE 46th Street at a curve after 0.8 mile. Pass NE 138th Avenue at 1.1 miles. The roadwalk becomes shadier. You reach CR 314 at Martin's Store ("Bent & Dent") after 2.5 miles. Turn left and continue another 2.6 miles south along the berm of CR 314 to Nuby's Corner, where you cross SR 40. The Florida Trail emerges from the woods on the left 2.2 miles south of the traffic light and follows the berm to cross the Ocklawaha River. It returns to the woods at the Marshall Swamp Trailhead, for a total of 12.6 miles of roadwalk from NE 145th Avenue until the trail is completed.

Bear Swamp Trail

Begin: Salt Springs Recreation Area
End: Salt Springs Recreation Area
Distance: 1.3 miles
Trail Difficulty: Easy
Highlights: Truly ancient cypresses, large lyonia shrubs
Hazards: Insects in summer
Trail Connections: None
Season: Year-round
Maps: None
Trailhead: From the Salt Springs Visitor Center along SR 19 in the Ocala National Forest, drive south 0.5 mile to the entrance to the Salt Springs Recreation Area on the left. Enter and pay your day use fee of $4.50 per person. Turn left and follow the road into the campground. Turn right on the first one-way lane leading away from you. Turn right and follow the one-lane road along the edge of the campground until you come to a parking area on the left. Park and walk over to the trailhead sign, next to a building.

Little known except to those who frequent this beautiful campground in the Salt Springs Recreation Area, the Bear Swamp Trail provides a glimpse into the ancient forest that undoubtedly crowded the shores of Salt Springs when botanist and explorer William Bartram visited the "amazing crystal fountain" in 1774. Start by walking down to the kiosk. Turn right and keep left at the fork as you walk through a hardwood forest with hickory, dogwood, elm, and oak. Massive southern magnolias tower overhead. As you meander along the path, elements of the Big Scrub appear—tall, slender loblolly pines and rusty and shiny lyonia. After 0.4 mile, you pass through a grove of tall straight loblolly pines.

At 0.6 mile, the boardwalk appears, ushering you into Bear Swamp. Birdcalls echo through the trees as you walk in dense shade and discover the object of this quest: an ancient cypress, close enough to touch, with a girth a good nine feet around. Look straight up, and you can see that the crown has broken off this monster of a tree, no doubt a sacrifice to a hurricane in the past. How did this cypress survive logging? Its surface is flawed and lumpy from massive galls, which would not go well through the sawmill.

As you continue a few more feet down the boardwalk, you can see another giant cypress in the distance—taller and even more magnificent than the first. Well up its trunk, it has a huge gaping crack down the center, the perfect place for an army of raccoons to hide. A branch that comes out above the hole is thicker around than the girth of any of the trees surrounding this one in the forest. Continue a little farther, and you'll see a third ancient cypress off to the right. It's humbling to be in the presence of such giants.

The boardwalk ends, and you continue your walk through mixed hardwood and scrub forest, passing a natural "container garden" of resurrection fern atop a snag as you wander beneath the shade of lyonia and southern magnolias en route back to the campground, completing the loop at the kiosk at 1.3 miles. Turn right to exit.

Buck Lake Loop Trail

Begin: Buck Lake Campground
End: Buck Lake Campground
Distance: 1.8 miles
Trail Difficulty: Easy
Highlights: Views of Buck Lake, tall pines
Hazards: None
Trail Connections: Florida Trail, State Road 19 to Juniper Springs
Season: Late fall–spring
Maps: No map available
Trailhead: From the Seminole Ranger Station in Umatilla, drive north on SR 19 for 10.1 miles to FR 595. Turn left on FR 595 and follow it for 2.4 miles to FR 514. Turn left on FR 514 and follow it for 0.5 mile to Buck Lake Campground. Veer right at the campground split and drive a short distance to the Buck Lake boat ramp and turnaround.

This hike circles Buck Lake, a ninety-acre natural lake. Buck Lake is deeper than most area lakes and has less prairie environment on its shores. Here the forest grows close to the water. On the lake's west side, the trail stays far above the lake on the surrounding hills. Depart the boat ramp area to intersect the Florida Trail and head south on the FT through sand pine scrub. Leave the FT and follow the loop trail back around the south side of the lake. The final part of the hike cuts through the Buck Lake Campground.

Walk away from the sandy boat ramp just a short distance to an old auto turnaround. Look for the blue blazes entering the woods to the left. Walk through sand pine woods with a thick understory to intersect the Florida Trail at 0.1 mile. Turn left on the FT and follow the orange blazes south. There are good vistas of the lake to your left through the low scrub. The exposed trailbed is often loose sand.

At 0.5 mile a side trail leads left, downhill to the lake. Dead sand pine snags extend to the sky overhead. These snags are important nesting and feeding sites for wildlife. The forest canopy thickens overhead and at trail level before coming to a trail junction at 1.0 mile. Turn left, leaving the Florida Trail, and follow the blue-blazed loop trail north into a tall stand of mixed pines towering overhead.

An old jeep trail soon comes in from the left—stay right and keep north on the wide path. Enter the east spur of the campground at mile 1.3. The sites here are shaded by tall pines. Lake level shoreline views open up before you reach the north campground spur at mile 1.6. Turn left at the north campground spur and complete your loop at mile 1.8.

Clearwater Lake Loop Trail

Begin: Clearwater Lake swim beach
End: Clearwater Lake swim beach
Distance: 1.1 mile
Trail Difficulty: Easy
Highlights: Lake views, fire ecology
Hazards: None
Trail Connections: None
Season: Late fall–spring
Maps: National forest handout
Trailhead: From the Seminole Ranger Station in Umatilla, drive north on SR 19 for 1.5 miles to CR 42. Turn right on CR 42, then head east for 6.3 miles to Clearwater Lake Recreation Area. The trailhead is near the swim beach on the lake.

This short loop hike circles Clearwater Lake. It stays close enough to the water to afford appealing long-range vistas. Along the way it passes through some burned pine woods. This may sound unappealing, but the walk provides insight into the how fire maintains Florida's pine forests.

Step onto the lake swim beach, then turn left, entering the woods on a yellow-blazed path. Leave the campground area behind. Swing around a cove beneath a mixed forest of pine and oak. Clearwater Lake is off to your right.

At 0.2 mile enter the burned-over area. The pine forest has been very open since the understory brush was burned down. It is now returning. First, fires return important nutrients for use by the more mature pines, which can resist most fires. Second, lack of fires allows other trees to grow, which changes the forest composition, making it less conducive for pine growth. Notice the blackened logs lying about on the ground; these decay and feed the standing trees.

At 0.5 mile, walk between the lake on your right and a young oak forest to your left. The swim beach is across the lake. Swing around another cove and turn toward the beach. To your left is a small pond. Cross a wet area on the first of two boardwalks at 0.8 mile. The campground is once again to your left. At 1.1 mile come to the swim beach again, completing the loop.

Juniper Run Nature Trail

Begin: Juniper Springs
End: Fern Hammock Springs
Distance: 0.5 mile
Trail Difficulty: Easy
Highlights: Bubbling springs, historic site
Hazards: Insects, poison ivy
Trail Connections: Florida Trail, Juniper Springs to Hopkins Prairie
Season: Year-round
Maps: Ocala National Forest map
Trailhead: From I-75, take exit 352, Ocala, and head east on SR 40. After 31 miles, the entrance to Juniper Springs Recreation Area is on the left. The nature trail starts at the waterwheel at the far side of the main spring.

This short trail packs a lot of punch in its half-mile length. Start at the renowned Juniper Springs and see the waterwheel erected by the Civilian Conservation Corps to provide electricity for the campground in the 1930s. Then walk along Juniper Creek to Fern Hammock Spring, an unusual natural collection of springs. This area can be busy on weekends, especially when the weather is warm.

Leave the parking area and walk to Juniper Springs. The main spring is a popular swimming hole and home to the American eel, a species that spawns at sea and returns inland via the St. Johns River and Juniper Run to live here. The walking trail starts on the far side of the waterwheel in a lush hammock of palms and oaks. Follow the new boardwalk that winds along the spring run, and marvel at the small bubbling springs beneath the glass-clear surface of the water. The outflow of Fern Hammock Springs joins with Juniper Springs to create Juniper Run, a popular paddling route through the Juniper Prairie Wilderness.

As you walk along Juniper Creek, several observation points give a closer glimpse of the clear stream. Live oaks tower overhead. Watch for small blonde-colored squirrels in the trees. They are a unique genetic mutation of gray squirrels and have been seen for generations in this very spot. At 0.5 mile you come to the outflow from Fern Hammock Springs. Turn left and walk up the arched footbridge. Look down to

Figure 15. Juniper Run Nature Trail travels through a lush semitropical forest. Photo by Sandra Friend

see turtles drifting through the clear water. Some of the springs look like pools of turquoise and gray paint, and some of them boil like sandstorms. Other trails lead back to the parking area, but you must cut through the campground to get there. Instead, backtrack along the nature trail and enjoy the semitropical forest and crystalline spring run on your return trip.

Lake Eaton Sinkhole Trail

Begin: FR 79 parking area
End: FR 79 parking area
Distance: 1.7-mile loop
Trail Difficulty: Moderate
Highlights: Deep sinkhole, Big Scrub
Hazards: Slippery boardwalk steps, insects
Trail Connections: Lake Eaton Trail
Season: Fall–spring
Maps: Ocala National Forest map, trail handout
Trailhead: From I-75 exit 352, Ocala, drive east on SR 40 for 13.4 miles to the Ocala National Forest. Turn left onto CR 314 and drive 9 miles north to FR 86, on your right just north of NE 172nd Ave. Follow this sand road for 1 mile to FR 79. Turn right and watch for the parking area on the left.

This loop trail passes through a mature sand pine scrub forest, characteristic of the high sandy ridges of the Big Scrub. It drops down to the Lake Eaton Sinkhole, a depression in the ridge harboring plant species unlike those in the surrounding woodlands. A boardwalk leads into the sinkhole for an unusual Florida trailside view—from the bottom looking up. A 0.5-mile shortcut trail bisects the main loop by cutting through the heart of the sand pine scrub to the sinkhole.

Leave the Lake Eaton trailhead and enter the forest. When you come to a kiosk with a trail map, turn right. You quickly arrive at the shortcut leading directly to the sinkhole to the left. Stay right, on the main loop, passing beneath a canopy of mature sand pines, with Chapman oaks, myrtle oaks, sand live oaks, and palmettos filling the understory. The northbound trail exhibits some significant elevation change as it journeys down toward the sinkhole. Pass a bench at 0.4 mile before turning westward on a carpet of sand, pine needles, and leaves.

The canopy briefly disappears after a mile. Off to your right are younger sand pines. You reenter the forest canopy before rejoining the Shortcut Trail at mile 1.2. Take a few more steps forward, and look out over the Lake Eaton Sinkhole. It's 122 feet deep and over 460 feet wide. Turn right and begin descending on a boardwalk into the sinkhole, where slightly cooler temperatures and moister ground support live oaks, magnolias, and cabbage palms on the slopes. Return by climbing the 119 steps back to the sandy ridge.

Turn right and you soon pass an informative kiosk. Erosion causes sinkholes as slightly acidic rainwater trickles through the sand to the bedrock and erodes the very porous limestone, forming a cavern. When the cavern collapses, either from water pressure from below or weight of materials above, it creates a sinkhole. Many sinkholes intersect the water table, but this one, in the dry Big Scrub, does not.

As you continue back to the parking lot, the trail is surrounded by sand pine scrub. Turn right at the trail map kiosk to exit.

Lake Eaton Trail

Begin: FR 79 parking area
End: FR 79 parking area
Distance: 2.1-mile loop
Trail Difficulty: Easy
Highlights: Sand pine scrub forest, lake views
Hazards: Poison ivy, insects
Trail Connections: Lake Eaton Sinkhole Trail
Season: Late fall–early spring
Maps: Ocala National Forest map, trail handout
Trailhead: From I-75 exit 352, Ocala, drive east on SR 40 for 13.4 miles to the Ocala National Forest. Turn left onto CR 314 and drive 9 miles north to FR 86, on your right just north of NE 172nd Ave. Follow this sand road for 1 mile to FR 79. Turn right and watch for the parking area on the left.

This trail loops down from a ridgeline sand pine scrub forest to the thickly wooded shores of Lake Eaton, a natural 380-acre lake. From the three overlooks at the water's edge you can see coffee-colored waters extending to the forest on the far shore. On the return trip, the path has more ups and downs, which is atypical of Florida hiking.

Leave the Lake Eaton trailhead and immediately cross FR 79. Just as quickly, you reenter the woods and descend through pine scrub, with tall sand pines forming the canopy. Around you are the oaks of the scrub—Chapman oaks, sand live oaks, and myrtle oaks. Below you are palmettos and green spongy lichens, known as deer moss. Deer moss is brittle when dry, but after a rain it absorbs moisture readily, then softens.

Soon you will come to the beginning of the loop. Turn right and continue descending while heading west. Pass a bench, and then cross an old forest road at 0.3 mile. The trail veers north and enters an area with young live oaks. Pass a second bench, then an unmarked junction at 0.6 mile. Stay left and begin heading into an area with large live oaks and tall slash pines overhead.

Come to the first boardwalk at 0.8 mile. Follow this wooden walkway out to Lake Eaton. Notice the maple trees and other deciduous trees, such as sweetgum and Florida hickory, dominant in the floodplain forest along the shoreline. Return to the main trail and walk parallel to the shore of Lake Eaton. Soon you come to a side trail to a second boardwalk. This one runs along the shore of the lake before returning to the main trail. The final boardwalk, at mile 1.2, overlooks a marsh.

The main trail goes north a short distance before veering sharply left into the sand pine scrub forest as you ascend the hill. The trail enters a spindly stand of sand pine at mile 1.7. At mile 2.1, you complete the loop. Turn right and backtrack uphill, crossing FR 79 to return to the trailhead.

Lake George Trail

Begin: Silver Glen Springs
End: Lake George
Distance: 1.2 miles
Trail Difficulty: Easy
Highlights: Fabulous views
Hazards: Mosquitoes, poison ivy
Trail Connections: The Yearling Trail across SR 19
Season: Fall–spring
Maps: Ocala National Forest map, trail handout
Trailhead: From Ocala, drive east on SR 40 for 33 miles to SR 19. Turn left on SR 19 and follow it for 5.8 miles to Silver Glen Springs. Turn right and follow the entrance road to the parking area. The Lake George Trail starts near the shaded picnic area.

This trail leaves the attractive and busy Silver Glen Springs and travels east through a mature high-canopied forest. The forest contains some near-record-size slash pines and pond pines along the way to Lake George, the broadest section of the chain of lakes that is the St. Johns River. There are three overlooks on the expansive body of water, where you may see alligators.

Leaving the shaded picnic area, you pass beneath a stand of ancient cedars growing along the edge of a line of Timucuan middens along Silver Glen Run. These ancient heaps of shells indicate human presence at the spring for more than three thousand years. After you cross the service road, notice the loblolly pines at 0.3 mile, towering more than a hundred feet tall. Massive live oaks provide shade.

The sandy trail bisects several culverts, which serve as wet weather drainages. Look for some large buckeye trees. This locale is near the southern limit of the buckeye's range. At 0.7 mile, come to the side trail to the first overlook. Take the 0.1-mile side trail right, to the shore of Lake George. Live oaks and palms form a frame for you to enjoy the view.

Back on the main trail, the path curves to the right through a patch of bamboo and pops out along the shoreline. Here a sign brags about the size of the lake. It is 5 miles wide, 19 miles long, and averages ten feet in depth. Mats of hydrilla drift past, and if you look closely, you'll notice the alligators. Affording great views, the trail follows the edge of Lake George to a final overlook, where there are benches for resting. A boathouse sits off in the distance, a relic from the past. Turn around and retrace your steps to the trailhead.

After your return trip, check out the Silver Glen Springs and the Spring Boils Trail. The short path starts on the far side of the Silver Glen Springs from the Lake George trailhead. It leads a quarter mile through a floodplain forest to a boardwalk running beside a clear stream. At the end of the boardwalk are the boils, noted in Marjorie Kinnan Rawlings's book *The Yearling* as "Jody's Spring." Water pushes up from the aquifer through the sand, giving it the appearance of boiling up from the earth.

Salt Springs Spur Trail

Begin: Salt Springs Marina Road
End: Florida Trail northwest of Hopkins Prairie
Distance: 2.7 miles
Trail Difficulty: Moderate
Highlights: Ponds and prairies
Hazards: Some sun exposure
Trail Connections: Florida Trail, Hopkins Prairie to Salt Springs Island
Season: Late fall–spring
Maps: Ocala National Forest map
Trailhead: From Ocala, drive east on SR 40 for 12 miles, then turn left on CR 314 and follow it for 18 miles to SR 19. Turn left on SR 19 and follow it 0.1 mile to Salt Springs Marina Road, FR 22. Turn right on FR 22 and follow it 100 yards to the trailhead on your right.

This path connects the Salt Springs Recreation Area with the Florida Trail between Lake Kerr and Hopkins Prairie. Cross busy SR 19, then enter a little-used area of the forest, passing small ponds and prairies. The sounds of civilization are left behind as you get deeper into the broken woods to access the Florida Trail. The Salt Springs Spur Trail does bisect a few jeep trails, but this does not detract from the mixture of sand pine scrub and wetlands.

Start the connector trail by following a blue-blazed path south from the parking area into a live oak forest. Watch for a small collapsed concrete structure on your left. The path roughly parallels SR 19 to your right, emerging alongside SR 19 at 0.2 mile. Turn left, paralleling the road on the edge of the woods for 0.2 mile. Look for the blue blazes across the road.

Cross SR 19 and pass through a fence and pass a sign that says "Ocala Trail, Spur." Enter a mixed pine woodland with an open understory. You are now following an old road that meanders southwest. Notice the abundance of turkey oaks. Turkey oaks are so named because the leaf resembles a turkey track. In open areas, also notice the prickly pear cactus, which grows in sandy, well-drained soils.

At 1.0 mile, pass between two small ponds surrounded by prairies. The canopy is open overhead as you swing around a pond, then turn sharply right into a woodland of longleaf pine underlain with numerous turkey oaks and grass.

Cross a little-used jeep trail at mile 1.5. Continue southward on high ground, passing a nearly pure stand of turkey oaks. Cross another faint road at mile 2.0. Descend slightly and come straight to a large prairie. Veer left and skirt around the pond-pocked grassland. Look for wading birds in the water. Turn left at the head of the prairie and enter a sandy young forest. The trail here was used as a fire line at some point. The forest on your left is much younger than the forest to your right.

Cross a third jeep trail at mile 2.5. Keep following the blue blazes across another jeep trail to intersect the Florida Trail at mile 2.7. From here, it is 2.5 miles north on the FT to FR 88 at Salt Springs Island and 5.8 miles south to the Hopkins Prairie campground.

Salt Springs Trail

Begin: Salt Springs Trailhead
End: Salt Springs Run Overlook
Distance: 1 mile one way
Trail Difficulty: Easy
Highlights: View of Salt Springs Run, diversity of habitats
Hazards: Insects, poison ivy
Trail Connections: None
Season: Fall–spring
Maps: Ocala National Forest map, trail handout
Trailhead: From Ocala, drive east on SR 40 for 12 miles, then turn left on CR 314 and follow it for 18 miles to SR 19. Turn right on SR 19 and follow it for 0.6 mile to the Salt Springs trailhead, which is on your left.

This trail leads from the Big Scrub of the Ocala National Forest down to Salt Springs Run, which is the outflow of Salt Springs. As the path heads downhill it reaches a loop that leads you through sand pine scrub, hardwood uplands, and a floodplain forest. A spur at the other end of the loop ends up at a boardwalk and observation platform overlooking Salt Springs Run. You can use the loop to maximize the number of habitats you see.

Florida has more than three hundred major springs. Twenty-seven of them are so-called first-magnitude springs, accounting for one third of all the first-magnitude springs in the United States. The mineral content of these springs varies, many containing calcium and magnesium. Salt Springs is noted for its salt content, tapped from ancient seas.

As you leave the parking area, the trail is a wide pathway into the sand pine scrub. Young oaks dominate the understory, and the sand pines provide a little shade. After you pass the trailhead kiosk you come to a split in the trail at 0.2 mile. Stay right—the other part of the loop is your return route. As you descend toward the run, moisture-loving trees such as Florida dogwood and southern magnolia line the path.

The trail reaches a T-intersection at 0.7 mile with a large sign showing the distance to the observation platform and the parking lot. Turn right and walk down a broad path between loblolly pines. The trail then enters a bayhead, where the footpath may be wet, and reaches a boardwalk through the floodplain forest of red maples, cabbage palms, and sweetgum. Beware of large poison ivy overhead mimicking hickory leaves. At the end of the boardwalk is an observation platform with a bench. Beyond you is the wide stream of Salt Springs Run. Get here early in the morning or late in the evening to enhance your chance of seeing wildlife.

Backtrack from the platform and stay right to return on the remainder of the loop trail. Pass an old road leading left as the trail climbs up into the Big Scrub. At the end of the loop, turn right and walk the last 0.2 mile back to the trailhead.

St. Francis Interpretive Trail

Begin: St. Francis trailhead
End: St. Francis trailhead
Distance: 7.3-mile loop with a 2.8-mile option
Trail Difficulty: Moderate
Highlights: Human history, boiling spring, variety of habitats
Hazards: Many unmarked turns, hunting season, insects
Trail Connections: None
Season: Fall–spring
Maps: Ocala National Forest map, trail handout, Florida Trail Association map
Trailhead: From the Seminole Visitor Center in Umatilla, drive north on SR 19 for 1.5 miles to CR 42. Turn right on CR 42 and head east for 18.1 miles to FR 542, where there is a sign for River Forest Group Camp and St. Francis Interpretive Trail. Turn left on FR 542 and follow it for 0.2 mile to the St. Francis trailhead on your left.

This trail parallels a side channel of the St. Johns River, the St. Francis Dead River, through a variety of interesting habitats en route to the former riverside settlement of St. Francis. Once a thriving river town connected to the outside world by steamboat traffic, St. Francis was a trading post where timber and citrus were exchanged for finished goods used by area settlements. Once the railroads laid rails through nearby Deland, steamboat shipping died off. By 1935 St. Francis was abandoned. Although the forests have reclaimed the area, you can still see evidence of the old settlements along this hike.

Start your hike by leaving the trailside kiosk and following the blue blazes west. Soon you cross a small creek on a palmetto log footbridge, hand-hewn and placed by Florida Trail Association volunteers years ago. Just past here, the regular undulations in the ground are remnants of row crop cultivation. The trail enters a forest thick with sweetgum and red maple trees. At 0.4 mile, you come to the first of many boardwalks that traverse wet areas of the forest. The wet flatwoods have yielded to a hammock of oaks and cabbage palms.

A bridge and boardwalk over a creek precede the junction with the lower end of the Yellow Loop at mile 1.1. Turn left here, following the yellow blazes. You soon come to another footbridge spanning a small stream. Just upstream of the footbridge is Rattlesnake Spring. The sulfurous water bubbles up from the ground through the sand. Check this out up close!

The path passes through wet areas and a boardwalk and then veers to the north to intersect the St. Francis Trail at mile 1.6. This is your decision point: turn right to take the shortcut along the 2.8-mile Yellow Loop, or turn left to continue along the main trail, following the blue blazes. The pine forest is much more open here. Be careful, since the trail flirts with jeep trails—watch for the next blue blaze as you cross a couple of boardwalks.

Come to an old logging railroad grade at mile 2.1. The footpath is arrow straight and offers views far ahead. With all the vegetation, today it's hard to imagine a train coming through here. Off to your left, on the far side of the small canal, the forest elevation rises up to sand pine scrub. At mile 2.6 the trail once again skirts and eventually crosses a jeep road. Meander north through open slash pine flatwoods and low palmetto. The trees are widely spaced, and the sun can blare down. Briefly traverse an oak strand while crossing a stream at mile 3.3 and then enter a denser stand of young pines.

Emerge onto a jeep road at 3.6 miles and turn right. This is the old Paisley–St. Francis Wagon Road. The Alexander Springs Wilderness is off to your left. Stay forward, following the blue blazes. This road leads straight to the St. Johns River a short way off. The buildings of St. Francis once lined this road, and the steamboat dock was at the end of the road on the river. Before you head to the river, watch on the right for the blue blazes leaving the road at mile 4.0. After visiting the old dock site, backtrack from the river to those blue blazes to enter an oak and palm hammock.

Soon you will see on your left a noisy water spigot emitting water beneath a live oak. The spigot has been stuck into an artesian spring and flows continuously. The wide path heads south along the St. Francis Dead River and splits at mile 4.4. To your left, a side trail leads a short distance down to the water. To your right, the blue-blazed St. Francis Trail now follows an old dike erected to flood the land for rice cultivation. The dike forms a division: you have floodplain forest to the left and pine flatwoods to the right. Follow the trail south down the dike until it comes to a stream meander at 4.9 miles. Span the stream on a log footbridge and briefly enter the pines before returning to the floodplain forest, where the footpath may be muddy.

Skirt another pine plantation at mile 5.6. You'll cross another boardwalk before coming to a trail junction. The upper Yellow Loop is just a few steps to your right. Stay left with the blue blazes, heading toward River Forest in a hammock of cabbage palm and oaks. Cross a small stream on a plank bridge before intersecting the lower Yellow Loop at mile 6.2. Continue forward along the route you first hiked on this journey, retracing your steps to the trailhead to complete the loop at mile 7.3.

The Yearling Trail

Begin: SR 19 trailhead
End: SR 19 trailhead
Distance: 5.5-mile loop with 3.5-mile option
Trail Difficulty: Moderate
Highlights: Historic early settlement points of interest
Hazards: Heat and sun, insects
Trail Connections: Florida Trail, Juniper Springs to Hopkins Prairie; Lake George Trail across SR 19
Season: Late fall–spring
Maps: Posted at trailhead and shown on Florida Trail Ocala North map
Trailhead: From Ocala, drive east on SR 40 for 33 miles to SR 19, just east of Juniper Springs Recreation Area. Turn left on SR 19 and follow it for 6.2 miles to the trailhead, marked by the "Yearling Trail" sign on the left across from Silver Glen Springs Recreation Area.

Pat's Island is a little piece of the long human history of the Ocala National Forest, romanticized in Marjorie Kinnan Rawlings's novel *The Yearling*. Reuben Long homesteaded here in the piney woods surrounded by the desertlike scrub. His descendants continued to raise cattle and children here until the government bought them out to create the Ocala National Forest in 1908. *The Yearling* captured the feel of life on Pat's Island during pioneer days, thanks to Rawlings's long visits with Calvin Long, who reminisced about his days raising a deer in the scrub. The novel was later made into a movie starring Gregory Peck, and the movie was actually filmed at this site. Pat's Island is now part of the Juniper Prairie Wilderness. This trail leads you through the wilderness and past several points of interest, including a cattle dip, a large sinkhole, the Long Cemetery, and homestead sites.

Start your hike at the kiosk and head west into the open scrub. This area suffered from an out-of-control prescribed burn nearly a decade ago and there are still snags in the path. But the young pines are growing up, and they are perfect for Florida scrub jays, which you may see along this part of the hike. After 0.8 mile, you come to the "Jody's Trace" sign. Turn right and follow the yellow blazes. You have reached Pat's Island.

The blazes lead you through into a dense stand of longleaf pine. At 1.2 miles you come across a concrete trough set into the ground. This was a cattle dip that Calvin Long used back when the government required that all cattle be dipped in an arsenic-based solution to kill ticks. The trail follows the edge of the island, with scrub surrounding you as you come to the next point of interest, the foundation of an old homestead. Following the yellow blazes, you arrive at an intersection with the Cross Trail. To the left it leads directly to the Long Cemetery and the exit for the loop. Turn right to walk the longer loop. In a few moments you see the sinkhole. It is on your left and drops over a hundred feet. Concrete sandbags and timbers support one side of the sinkhole. There is a less steep access to the bottom of the sinkhole on the far side from the trail. This is a dry sinkhole, but the settlers once used it as a water source, as water seeped out of the water table onto the rocks.

Where the trail forks at the next interpretive marker, stay to the left, walking beneath the sand pines. At mile 2.5 you reach the Florida Trail. To your right it heads to the Pat's Island trailhead and Hopkins Prairie. Turn left into the Juniper Prairie Wilderness and follow the trail past a dry campsite and beneath an ancient dogwood tree. You reach the next trail junction with the yellow blazes at 3.2 miles. Turn left. A little way up on the right is a cistern, the last remnant of Reuben Long's homestead. A few minutes later you come to the Long Cemetery, where the pioneers who lived on Pat's Island are buried. As you exit the small cemetery, continue straight along the cross trail. Turn right at the sign. You are now following an old wagon road past the remains of two more homesteads, where only the clearings and small shards of glass and plates provide a clue that people once lived here—the families of Calvin and Cora Long. This is where many scenes from the movie *The Yearling* were filmed.

Continue through the longleaf pines and you reach the other side of the "Jody's Trace" sign at 4.7 miles. Leaving Pat's Island, the trail makes a beeline through the open scrub back to the trailhead, ending after 5.5 miles.

Timucuan Nature Trail

Begin: Alexander Springs Recreation Area
End: Alexander Springs Recreation Area
Distance: 0.9-mile loop
Trail Difficulty: Easy; partially wheelchair accessible
Highlights: A broad variety of habitats in a very short distance
Hazards: Insects, poison ivy
Trail Connections: Florida Trail, Clearwater Lake to Alexander Springs
Season: Year-round
Maps: On trailhead kiosk
Trailhead: From SR 40 east of Astor, turn south on CR 445A and follow the signs. After 0.4 mile, turn left on CR 445 and continue south for 5.7 miles to the recreation area entrance on the right, just after the bridge over Alexander Springs Creek. A $4 per person entrance fee applies.

Walk through the concession area down a concrete path to Alexander Spring, a sparkling first-magnitude spring. At the edge of the spring turn right and follow the path over to the trailhead. A boardwalk leads into a lush hydric hammock, deeply shaded by cabbage palms that grow in profusion in the shallow waters surrounding the spring. Clusters of cinnamon ferns rise from patches of land between clear, sand-bottomed rivulets. You feel as if you've walked into a lush jungle, and so it was for the Timucua who once lived along the banks of this spring. Interpretive signs relate information about the habitat and its inhabitants.

You come to a junction with a rough sand footpath. Follow the footpath as it climbs up into an upland forest, where dogwood, oaks, and magnolia grow on a high bluff along a flowing creek. A red-shouldered hawk wheels overhead. The trail drops down to cross the creek, making a curve to the left into the deep dark shade of a palm hammock to cross a long boardwalk across a crystalline stream. On the other side of the boardwalk, roots invade the footpath and the soil may be squishy. The trail rises back into the upland forest and continues to ascend into the Big Scrub, where gnarled sand live oaks provide shade beneath the tall sand pines. The sweet aroma of silk bay fills the air, and seafoam streamers of old man's beard dangle from the twisted branches of a rusty lyonia. The air is thick with humidity rising from the lush undergrowth.

As the trail drops down out of the scrub, it enters another grove of extremely tall cabbage palms. Dark green needle palms fill the understory. You reach another boardwalk at 0.4 mile, where a stand of ancient cypress reminds you of the passage of time between the era of the Timucua and the bathers in the spring today. A side trail leads off to the right to a small sinkholelike depression. As the trail swings to the left, you can hear the playful laughter of children splashing in the spring. Dropping into a forest of magnolia trees, the trail curves left and the air gets heavier and damper—you know the spring is close.

At 0.6 mile, the trail meets a boardwalk at a T. Turn right to take a short trip down to the boardwalk's end, where an observation platform on Alexander Run gives you a sweeping view of the waterway as it comes around the curve. Turn around and follow the boardwalk as it keeps close to the shore of the run. Another side trail leads to an observation deck. As you continue to walk in the deep shade beneath the cabbage palms, notice the crown of one palm dropping so low to the ground that you can touch it. The boardwalk crosses over forks of a flowing creek, where the hammock is younger, the understory tangled. One more crossing of a broad sand-bottomed stream, and you're at the end of the loop. Turn right to exit.

Hiking Trails of the Osceola National Forest

In the northeast corner of Florida, near the Georgia line, lies the Osceola National Forest. It is Florida's smallest national forest, yet it comes in at over 200,000 acres. And on this acreage is a sizable amount of open pine flatwoods, a fast disappearing ecosystem, since it is so easily developed. Interspersed throughout the pine flatwoods are swamps—watery areas full of cypress, black gum, and bay trees. One special area has been set aside—the Big Gum Swamp Wilderness, designated by Congress in 1984. Other parcels have natural lakes and streams that diversify the forest landscape, and it is these lands that an interesting segment of the Florida Trail traverses.

Here you access the FT at Olustee Battlefield. This preserved Civil War site is where Florida's largest Civil War altercation took place, in February of 1864. And to this day, there is an annual battle reenactment. The FT continues beyond the battlefield as a well-marked and maintained pathway, coursing through palmetto thickets beneath tall longleaf pines—the habitat of the red-cockaded woodpecker. I have seen and heard this bird more in the Osceola than anywhere in my Florida travels.

The Florida Trail also passes by Ocean Pond, a large lake in the forest. Cypress swamps are never far away, and the FT takes you by and occasionally over them via elaborate boardwalks. There is even a trail shelter for overnight hikers here. On down the line are elevated paths, leftovers from the old logging rail trams of a century ago, passing more cypress swamps and crossing slow-moving creeks. Fire is a critical element of the pine flatwoods, and you will undoubtedly see its effects here. Before exiting at Deep Creek trailhead, the Florida Trail winds beneath tall live oaks and laurel oaks.

Another trail of note makes a loop through the 13,000-acre Black Gum Swamp Wilderness. This path is less well maintained, offering a challenging hike through bear habitat that was once the domain of the logging and turpentine industry.

Trail Updates at a Glance

- The Southeast Black Gum Swamp Wilderness Trail has been permanently closed.

Florida Trail, Olustee Battlefield to Turkey Run

Begin: Olustee Battlefield
End: Turkey Run Trailhead
Distance: 9.7 miles
Trail Difficulty: Difficult when water is high
Highlights: Civil War battle site, trail shelter
Hazards: Wet trail
Trail Connections: Florida Trail, Turkey Run to Deep Creek; Ocean Pond Connector Trail
Season: Spring–fall
Maps: Florida Trail Osceola, Osceola National Forest map
Trailhead: From the Osceola Ranger Station, 12 miles east of Lake City on US 90, keep east on US 90 for 3.2 miles past the ranger station to the Olustee Battlefield. Turn left into the battlefield area and turn left again into a parking area just past the railroad tracks on your left.

This section of the Florida Trail is well marked, groomed, and maintained. Formerly known as the Osceola Trail, it starts out at the site of Florida's largest Civil War battlefield and heads into attractive pine flatwoods, passing occasional cypress depressions. It then keeps north and west, eventually coming to a welcome trail shelter on the banks of a waterway. This section of the Florida Trail ends shortly after the shelter, at the Turkey Run trailhead.

Leave the Olustee parking area and head north, crossing a boardwalk and passing through the Olustee Battlefield site, a state park, on a gravel road. In February, 1864, Union forces had taken Jacksonville and headed west to cut off Confederacy-bound food supplies from central Florida. Southern forces picked Olustee as a good defensive place, with Ocean Pond on one side and a deep swamp on the other. The opposing armies battled beneath the towering pines until dark, and the Union was forced to retreat eastward to Jacksonville. The state park provides picnic tables and a water spigot.

Today the Florida Trail winds beneath tall longleaf pines with a

Figure 16. Sunset at Ocean Pond. Photo by Johnny Molloy

mown grassy understory. This spot, first memorialized in 1913 by the Florida legislature, is used for the battle reenactment held every February. Beyond the battlefield site palmetto grows under the longleaf pines and the FT shares treadway with the Nice Wander Loop, a nature trail. Pass through a clearing and a wet area overlain with boardwalks then reach Forest Road 208 at 1.0 mile. Turn left on FR 208 and follow it for 0.4 mile—the Florida Trail then reenters the woods on road right. The forest here is young and offers less shade.

Come to a long boardwalk at mile 1.6 and reenter pine-palmetto flatwoods, swinging around a cypress head—a line of cypress bordering the uppermost portion of a drainage—on your left. Pass another cypress head at mile 2.2. Keep to the open flatwoods until oak woods are reached just before coming to Cobb Hunt Camp at mile 3.5. The FT meanders through the camp to intersect a logging berm at mile 3.7. Turn right. The berms of these logging tracks were raised so that trains could get through the often soggy forests. Laurel oak, pine, and bay complement the cypress trees. A boardwalk traverses the wettest section. Leave the berm at mile 4.3, making a sharp left, and come to FR 207A. Cross the road and enter a timbered section of forest, coming back to shady woods at mile 4.5. Swing around a marsh and a dug pond, then come to County Road 250A at mile 5.1. Take a few steps to the right along the road and step back into the woods. The Florida Trail reaches a junction at 5.4 miles. A blue-blazed path leads left 1 mile to Ocean Pond Campground.

Continue northwest through pine, bay, and palmetto woods, soon coming to FR 268, which also leads to Ocean Pond Campground. Keep forward and cross a long boardwalk over a cypress head. There are numerous bay trees in this area. Emerge onto FR 241 at mile 6.2. Turn right along the forest road to CR 250A. Turn left here and walk over the paved road to cross I-10, where the cars below are moving startlingly fast. Leave the high-speed world behind at the bottom of the bridge and dive left into the woods at mile 6.8. Soon cross FR 263B and begin a long stretch of open flatwoods. Come to a pine plantation at mile 7.7, and wind among the dense rows of shade-bearing evergreens, emerging onto CR 250A at mile 8.2. While crossing the road, you also bridge a creek below you.

Pass through an ATV-proof gate and parallel the stream, soon turning away from the water and resuming a westerly course through pine flatwoods. Watch for a pond off to your left at mile 8.6. Keep northwest, coming to a footbridge over a creek, and turn sharply right. Dead ahead is a trail shelter, at mile 9.3. This shelter has a wooden board floor, is open on all sides, and is covered with a tin roof supported by beams at the corners. A metal fire grate is nearby. Water can be obtained from the creek below and a vault toilet lies a short distance away.

To continue on the Florida Trail, backtrack just a short distance and continue northwesterly. The trail bisects a timber cut and then pine plantations, crossing another stream. Emerge onto CR 250 and the Turkey Run trailhead at 9.7 miles. It is 11.4 miles west on the Florida Trail to Deep Creek trailhead and the end of the FT through the Osceola National Forest.

Florida Trail, Turkey Run to Deep Creek

Begin: Turkey Run Trailhead
End: Deep Creek
Distance: 11.4   miles
Trail Difficulty: Moderate to difficult
Highlights: Swamp boardwalks, pine flatwoods, rail tram berms
Hazards: Wet walking when water is up
Trail Connections: Florida Trail, Olustee Battlefield to Turkey Run; West Tower Connector Trail
Season: Fall–spring
Maps: Florida Trail Osceola, Osceola National Forest map
Trailhead: From the Osceola Ranger Station, 12 miles east of Lake City on US 90, keep east on US 90 for 1.9 miles past the ranger station to CR 250A. Turn left on CR 250A and follow it for 7.2 miles to CR 250. Turn right on CR 250 and drive 0.1 mile to the Turkey Run trailhead, which is on your left. The Deep Creek end of the trail can be reached leaving Lake City at the junction of US 90 and US 441, heading north on US 441 for 11.1 miles to Drew Road. Turn right on Drew Road (it turns into FR 262), and follow it for 0.6 mile to the Deep Creek trailhead, on your right.

This section of the Florida Trail takes you through the northwesterly portion of the Osceola National Forest and crosses relatively few marked forest roads in the process. Leave Turkey Run trailhead and follow the orange blazes through classic pine flatwoods and along and sometimes through cypress swamps. The path is well marked, also traveling through palmetto plains and young woods. Pass West Tower Hunt Camp, which has potable water and a flush toilet. Continue north and west along the FT to end this section at Deep Creek trailhead.

Start your hike by leaving the Turkey Run trailhead past the large "Florida Trail" sign. Work your way around the edge of the parking area through a pine plantation across the undulating ground between the rows of trees. Quickly leave the plantation for pine-palmetto flatwoods and come to a little-used, grassy jeep trail at 0.2 mile. Turn left, joining the jeep track, and come to your first boardwalk at 0.6 mile. This boardwalk circumvents a swampy area. The next boardwalk passes over

Figure 17. Backpacker treks through palmettos in the Osceola National Forest. Photo By Johnny Molloy

a sluggish creek—look for the moving water. Traverse more boardwalks at mile 1.2 and 1.6.

The forest is mixed here, with pine flatwoods and cypress heads. In some places the two types of trees grow together. And where the pines grow alongside the cypress, look at bases of the pines—they too are buttressed, much like the cypress. These wide bases help keep the plants upright in the water. Just past the last boardwalk, leave the jeep trail and turn right into flatwoods. Soon cross a swamp on a long boardwalk, then walk a wet area to cross another boardwalk. Leave this cypress slough for a drier forest, passing another cypress slough at mile 3.1. A finger extension of this slough to your right must be navigated without benefit of a boardwalk.

Keep forward and merge into another pine plantation. The path here makes many twists and turns in the plantation before intersecting Forest Road 234 at mile 3.7. Turn right and stay along the road a short distance, before veering right and entering a palmetto plain. You do not cross the forest road. Meander through the open shadeless area before coming to and this time crossing FR 234, at mile 4.3. Pick up and trace a jeep trail through a shady pine forest.

Palmetto grows throughout the Osceola National Forest. It is the most easily recognizable shrub in the state. Its leaves are fan shaped, growing from a trunk that is often buried. Its fruit starts out yellowish, then turns black as it matures. Palmettos grow in a wide variety of conditions, including sandy prairies, dunes, flatwoods, and palm hammocks all over Florida. They also ranges up the east coast into Georgia and the Carolinas and are the northernmost palm species in North America. In former times palmetto leaves were used for making baskets, brooms, and hats.

Beyond FR 234, the Florida Trail circumvents one wet area then comes to a second, which is a slow creek. Turn left, crossing this creek on a boardwalk at mile 5.3. Stay with the jeep trail through a young longleaf plantation that soon gives way to taller woodland. Use a boardwalk to cross another cypress strand at mile 5.9. At mile 6.4, come to a trail junction. A blue-blazed trail leads forward 0.2 mile to West Tower Hunt Camp, where there is a water faucet. A nice camp in oaks is located on the left just a short distance down the blue-blazed path. The Florida Trail, however, turns right and crosses a boardwalk before intersecting FR 233 at mile 6.6.

Keep forward and immediately cross a creek on a boardwalk, continuing on an elevated rail tram berm, heading due north. Look for remains of crossties on the trail. These crossties were hand-hewn from cypress and heart of pine. Stay mostly in pine flatwoods, passing occasional low cypress and hardwood swamps on more boardwalks. Enter a pine plantation and watch for the undulating land under your feet.

At mile 7.9 leave the tram route and turn left on a four-wheel-drive track. Soon bisect the Red Trail, a horse path marked with red diamonds, which loops back to West Tower. At mile 8.9, make a brief detour on an easily missed boardwalk to the right of the jeep road, bypassing a wet area. Watch as the orange-blazed Florida Trail dives right, into attractive pine flatwoods interspersed with live and laurel oaks.

Enjoy live oak and pine trees before intersecting Forest Road 237 at mile 9.5. Cross the forest road and keep on through pine flatwoods. The trail turns and winds, attempting to stay on the highest ground, but it eventually has to span a wet area on a boardwalk. Here the trail turns north and west to join a power line clearing just before reaching the Deep Creek trailhead and FR 262 (Drew Road) at mile 11.4, the trailhead directions for which are given above.

Battleline Trail, Olustee Battlefield Historic State Park

Begin: Olustee Battlefield Visitor Center
End: Olustee Battlefield Visitor Center
Distance: 1.1-mile loop
Trail Difficulty: Wheelchair accessible with assistance
Highlights: Interpretive information that makes the battle come alive
Hazards: Insects
Trail Connections: Nice Wander Trail; Florida Trail
Season: Year-round
Maps: Posted at trailhead
Trailhead: From I-75 exit 427, Lake City, drive 18.6 miles east on US 90. Turn left to enter the park. Drive past the fire tower and park at the visitor center on the right. There is no fee to visit this park.

This path loops through the Olustee Battlefield Historic State Park, one Florida's first parks and now jointly operated by the Osceola National Forest and Florida State Parks. Follow this interpretive footpath to meander through both time and space at the site of the bloodiest battle in Florida history, an engagement February 20, 1864, near the end of the War Between the States on. Monuments and displays add to the aura of the site.

Start by walking through the visitor center to get a sense of why this battle occurred. General Truman Seymour had just captured Jacksonville. Eager to push to Tallahassee, Seymour started his troops westward down the railroad before he received orders from his superiors. War-weary but eager to defend the commerce routes, the Confederate Army was ready and waiting at Ocean Pond. As more than ten thousand men met on this spot, the battle unfolded in the piney woods.

The trail begins directly across the road at a kiosk explaining the scene of the battle. Continue past the bench to the first interpretive markers and bench. Turn right. Follow the broad trail beneath the longleaf pines. A red arrow on a silver diamond marks the trail. At the T-intersection, turn left. As you pass the interpretive markers, pause and learn how the

Figure 18. Monument to Confederate soldiers at Olustee Battlefield, site of Florida's most significant clash of the Civil War. Photo by Johnny Molloy

battle unfolded. Dense saw palmetto, bayheads, and the tall pines themselves all played a role in how the soldiers advanced and retreated. At the fork, stay left. Off to the right is the open field where most of the combat occurred as cavalry companies met. Today grandstands hold visitors during the annual reenactment, the largest such event in the Southeast.

The trail continues along an ecotone between scrubby flatwoods and pine flatwoods, where you see both prickly pear cactus and bracken fern, and more interpretive markers. At 0.5 mile, you pass a bench and the trail turns left. A bayhead swamp is off behind the pines on your right. During the battle it proved a fatal obstacle for retreating soldiers. Cross over a small bridge and reach another bench at an intersection. Continue straight, and cross a second intersection. The distant monument and flags come into view. The loop ends at another bench. Turn right and walk back to the visitor center. The Nice Wander Trail and the Florida Trail start at the trailhead beyond the fire tower.

Big Gum Swamp Wilderness Trail

Begin: Forest Road 232
End: Forest Road 232
Distance: 4.7-mile loop
Trail Difficulty: Difficult
Highlights: Big Gum Swamp, logging and turpentine history
Hazards: Losing the trail, bear habitat, insects
Trail Connections: None
Season: Fall–spring
Maps: Osceola National Forest map, National Forest handout
Trailhead: From the junction of US 90 and US 441 in Lake City, head north on US 441 for 11.1 miles to Drew Road. Turn right on Drew Road (it becomes FR 262 and a dirt road) and follow it for 9.1 miles. Turn left on FR 232 and drive just a few yards before coming to a grassy area on the right. Here is a post with a wilderness sign. Look also for the silver circular blaze on a tree behind the grassy area, marking the beginning of the trail.

This trail explores the wilds of the Big Gum Swamp Wilderness. It makes a loop mostly through the wilderness area, with its last segment along a forest road. The trail is very passable near the road on both ends. In the middle, however, the trail is overgrown and challenging to follow, so know this going in. Wilderness trails are generally maintained less than other trails, so that the experience retains a wild character. Take your time and follow the silver circular blazes that mark the path. Don't be surprised if the vegetation is over your head.

The trail loops through pine flatwoods and brushy burned-over areas, crossing a creek along a cypress slough. A century ago the pines in these woods were tapped for turpentine and logged, along with the cypress from the swamps. A discerning eye will spot the remains of old clay pots used to collect pine sap from the trees. Please leave these artifacts for others to discover and enjoy.

As you leave FR 232, head east into the pine flatwoods on an old logging tramway. At 0.3 mile, the trail splits; stay left, following the silver circular blazes as the trail leaves the tramway to follow an old logging road. After a mile the trail narrows down to barely a trace. Keep an eye on those blazes. The flatwoods get very wet, and you may wade in places. You emerge into an open palmetto plain with few trees and showing signs of a previous burn. The footpath is very overgrown.

After 1.9 miles, the trail makes a sharp left, leaving one roadbed for another. Pass alongside another palmetto field on your left. Stay with the trail through scattered trees as the path splits between the palmetto field on your left and one on your right. You come to an elevated berm at mile 2.3. Turn sharply right here on the old train bed, which has marshy depressions on both sides. These depressions were made when the soil was scooped out to construct the berm.

Walk the berm, leaving it at mile 2.5. Turn left, walk a few feet down an old roadbed, and turn left again, turning nearly 180 degrees from the direction you were walking on the berm. The trail becomes easier to follow. After 3.1 miles, you see the site of an old cabin on your right. The trail crosses a creek—expect wet feet—and continues along the edge of a cypress swamp and slough. On the far side of the slough is an attractive pine and oak forest.

These attractive woods give way to wet flatwoods with a lot of bay and pines before coming to FR 232 at mile 3.6. Turn left here and soon pass FR 272, coming in from your right. Keep heading southwest along FR 232, coming to the original trailhead and completing your loop at mile 4.7.

Fanny Bay Trail

Begin: I-10 westbound Sanderson rest area
End: Fanny Bay observation deck
Distance: 0.5 mile one way
Trail Difficulty: Wheelchair accessible with assistance
Highlights: Immersion in a swamp forest with giant cypresses
Hazards: Rest area traffic, mosquitoes
Trail Connections: None
Season: Year-round
Maps: On the interpretive sign at the gate
Trailhead: From the I-10 Sanderson exit, drive 6 miles west to the I-10 Sanderson rest area and park out front. The trail begins at the interpretive sign in front of the restrooms.

This recent addition to the trails of Osceola National Forest opens up access to a magical place just off the interstate—Fanny Bay, a natural swamp forest brimming with life. Start your walk at the vivid "Fanny Bay Trail" sign with the big frog in front of the restrooms. Follow the yellow frogs painted on the pavement through the breezeway and out along the sidewalk, crossing the truck parking area exit. Watch for traffic. The trail begins in earnest at a gate with an interpretive sign dominated by a big butterfly and a rough map of the route. The interpretive signs along this trail are unlike any I've ever seen—they are die-cut and stand out with bold photos and colors.

Turn left at the arrow and follow an old limerock forest road headed west, paralleling the interstate through a young pine plantation. The elevation rises slightly. At 0.3 mile you cross over a culvert. At an interpretive sign at a forest road junction, the trail turns right. Cattails flank the entrance to the boardwalk. The watery wilderness of Fanny Bay is a swamp forest with red maple, sweetgum, wax myrtle, and cypress. Pines line the drier ground on the edges. Water spangles float across the dark tannic water. You see old cypress stumps left behind by the loggers and pass one unusual double-trunked cypress on the right.

The trail ends at an observation platform with a bench at 0.5 mile and a "Wet and Wild Swamps" interpretive marker. Tall cypresses abound.

After you've had a good look, turn around to retrace your steps. Right in front of you is a grand old cypress that looks as if it would take five people holding hands to encircle the base. It's a perfect nesting place for the swallow-tailed kites that soar overhead.

As you walk back along the forest road, look for chips of old clay turpentine collecting cups embedded in the limerock. End your walk after 1.1 miles in front of the rest area building.

Mount Carrie Wayside Nature Trail

Begin: US 90 wayside
End: US 90 wayside
Distance: 1-mile loop
Trail Difficulty: Moderate
Highlights: Ancient pines and red-cockaded woodpeckers
Hazards: Easy to lose the trail in several places
Trail Connections: None
Season: Fall–spring
Maps: None
Trailhead: Drive 10 miles east of Lake City on US 90. The Mount Carrie Wayside will be on your left across from the Columbia Correctional Institution.

This interpretive trail immerses you in the longleaf pine ecosystem, a habitat that has all but vanished from private lands in the Southeast. The trail is a favorite destination for birders, since nesting red-cockaded woodpeckers can be seen from several points along the trail.

The trail begins by crossing a short boardwalk where moisture-loving plants such as hatpins and wild bachelor's button grow beneath the old growth longleaf pines. There are many interpretive signs along this trail, and silver diamond markers with the hiker symbol to guide you along. The understory is open beneath the longleaf pines, the view clear above the saw palmetto. After 0.2 mile, you pass a massive gopher tortoise burrow on the right, and the habitat shifts to turkey oak and sand live oak with scrub plants. You can see a railroad track off to your right in the forest. After you cross a firebreak at mile 0.4, there are white-banded trees ahead—the nesting trees for the red-cockaded woodpeckers. This is where it gets hard to follow the trail, since visitors have beaten many paths to the bases of the various nesting trees. Keep right at the fork and you'll arrive at "A Hole in One" interpretive sign at 0.5 mile. Turn left and you'll walk past the "Candle Trees" sign a few moments later. Take the time to inspect one of the banded trees and notice the dripping sap around the nest hole.

Making a sharp left at 0.6 mile, the trail now follows a broad jeep track under the pines. You can see the highway and prison complex in the distance on your right. Cross a jeep track junction and continue straight. At 0.8 miles, the trail leaves the jeep track by turning right and becoming a narrow footpath making a beeline through tall grasses. You complete the loop by emerging back at the wayside park.

Nice Wander Trail

Begin: US 90 trailhead
End: US 90 trailhead
Distance: 1.6-mile loop with shorter options
Trail Difficulty: Wheelchair accessible with assistance
Highlights: Red-cockaded woodpecker nests in ancient pines
Hazards: Insects
Trail Connections: Florida Trail, Olustee to Turkey Run; Battleline Trail
Season: Year-round
Maps: At trailhead kiosk and on Florida Trail Osceola Map
Trailhead: From I-75 exit 427, Lake City, drive 18.6 miles east on US 90. Turn left to enter Olustee Battlefield Historic State Park. Immediately turn left into the trailhead parking area adjoining US 90.

This new loop in the Florida Trail provides a prime place to see red-cockaded woodpeckers around their nest holes in ancient longleaf pines. It also is a firm natural surface suitable for motorized wheelchairs and for regular wheelchairs with assistance.

The trail starts at the kiosk. Cross the small boardwalk and follow the orange and white blazes toward the forest. The fire tower and Olustee Battlefield Visitor Center are off to your right. You pass a historic cemetery on the left. After the trail passes through a gate, it leaves the road to start down a footpath into the longleaf pine forest. The understory is open, with only scattered patches of saw palmetto. After 0.3 mile, the trees become denser. Listen closely, and you can hear the tap of woodpeckers on the wood. At 0.4 mile, you reach an intersection with a jeep road, and Loop A follows blue blazes to the right. Continue straight. The white-banded trees are where the red-cockaded woodpeckers live. This endangered species nests only in old growth longleaf pines at least a hundred years old. At 0.5 mile, look up into the trees to see the sap dripping from the nest hole areas; the woodpeckers peck holes to release sticky sap so as to protect the nest hole entrance from predators such as rat snakes. Loop B turns off to the right; continue straight. You can see a break in the trees off to the left where a seasonal marsh exists.

At 0.8 mile, the trail ascends a gently sloping boardwalk through a wet area with two benches for resting. Where the boardwalk ends, the orange blazes lead straight ahead—that's the main Florida Trail. Turn right here to follow the white blazes back along a forest road to the gate where the footpath through the forest began.

The Loop B crossover meets the forest road at 1.1 miles, and the Loop A crossover at 1.3 miles. Passing a "Horse Trailer Parking" sign and a cattle pen, you complete the loop. Continue down the white-blazed forest road through the gate, emerging from the cool shade of the oaks to reach trailhead at 1.6 miles.

Trampled Track Trail

Begin: Olustee Beach Recreation Area
End: Ocean Pond
Distance: 0.3-mile round trip
Trail Difficulty: Wheelchair accessible with assistance
Highlights: Beautiful floodplain forest along Ocean Pond
Hazards: Mosquitoes, slippery boardwalk
Trail Connections: None
Season: Year-round
Maps: None
Trailhead: Drive 15 miles east of Lake City on US 90 to the hamlet of Olustee. Turn left at the sign for Olustee Beach and proceed a short distance to the Olustee Beach Recreation Area on FR 231. The Trampled Track Trail starts toward the rear of the recreation area. There is a parking fee.

Starting around 1875, retired Union soldier Tom Russell and his business partner Isaac Eppinger bought up the land around Ocean Pond. The forest boomed with the sounds of longleaf pine and cypress being felled, and the sawmill hummed, cutting trees into lumber. The Trampled Track Trail follows part of the route of the old logging railroad that brought the felled timber to the sawmill.

Park near the recreation area restrooms and walk east toward the elaborate entryway to this short interpretive trail. The barrier-free old tram road provides solid footing. It is lined with netted chain and cinnamon ferns under the cool shade of large water oaks, loblolly pines and red maples. Bird songs echo through the trees, and you pass several interpretive markers about the sawmill and logging operations. A tall stand of longleaf pines is to your left as you approach a platform with a bench. Look out over the old logging railroad track, used by twenty-ton steam locomotives until 1930.

Turn left and step onto the boardwalk, which winds beneath the pines to reach the cypress-lined fringe of Ocean Pond. This is a lush and cool microclimate, dense with ferns. The trail ends at an overlook on Ocean Pond after less than 0.15 mile. During the height of timbering operations

Figure 19. The Trampled Track Trail follows an old railroad grade for part of its length. Photo by Sandra Friend

this massive body of water was where the logs floated, waiting to be put through the sawmill. Now you can look across the pristine lake and see the campground on the far side. Turn around and return the way you came, reaching the end of the trail at 0.3 mile.

Hiking Trails of
the Apalachicola National Forest

Florida's largest national forest is the Apalachicola National Forest. It encompasses a wide swath of the panhandle from Tallahassee to the Apalachicola River. Within these confines are sand hills, sinkholes, lakes, pinelands, blackwater streams, spring-fed ponds, rich swamps, and rivers. The vast amounts of water that flow through this land feed the rich estuaries of the Gulf. The flora along these waterways—cypress, black gum, titi, sweetbay magnolia, and more—filter and cleanse the water that goes on to nurture young fish and shellfish off the Florida coast. Tall longleaf pine woods mixed with oaks and occasional hardwood hammocks provide food and cover for animals and birds alike.

Within the forest are several unique areas. There are the savannas—grassy plains that are both flood and fire tolerant. Within these savannas are carnivorous flora, such as pitcher plants, that capture insects and absorb them as food. The Leon Sinks Geological Area is a hilly place of limestone sinkholes, some filled with clear water, others filled with moisture-loving trees. Creeks flow underground and appear above ground a distance later. The area has one of the largest underwater cave systems in the world. The Bradwell Bay Wilderness extends over nearly 25,000 acres of open pinelands and some of the deepest swamps in the entire forest, where old growth trees patiently live out the changing of the seasons.

Hikers can enjoy a sixty-five mile section of the Florida Trail, most of it in solitude. Here it passes through nearly every environment the Apalachicola has to offer. The pathway traverses longleaf flatwoods, hills cloaked in oaks, along the beautiful watershed of the Sopchoppy River, and across the deep swamps of Bradwell Bay. A sense of solitude continues in the western half of the forest where creeks abound, such as Coxes Branch. Visit the deserted turpentine community of Vilas and enter a place of hills and lakes and savannas before leaving the forest.

There are other trails besides the Florida Trail in the Apalachicola. The Wright Lake Trail makes a loop through nearly every ecosystem represented within the forest. The Sinkhole Trail tours the unusual Leon Sinks. The Gum Swamp Trail explores the hardwood swamps near Leon Sinks. The Trail of Lakes makes loop possibilities from the Camel Lake Recreation Area. And other nature trails round out mix of Apalachicola pathways that will not fail to enchant the forest visitor.

Trail Updates at a Glance

- The Trout Pond Recreation Area is now closed with no assurance that it will reopen

Florida Trail, Medart to Bradwell Bay

Begin: US 319 at Medart
End: Bradwell Bay Wilderness trailhead at FR 329
Distance: 12.7 miles
Trail Difficulty: Moderate
Highlights: Sopchoppy River walk, old growth magnolias, solitude
Hazards: Steep sandy ravines
Trail Connections: Florida Trail, Bradwell Bay to Porter Lake
Season: Fall–spring
Maps: Florida Trail Apalachicola East, Apalachicola National Forest map
Trailhead: From the Wakulla County Courthouse in Crawfordville, drive 8.2 miles south on US 319 to the Florida Trail Medart trailhead. It will be on your right. There is a parking area here.

This hike starts at the southeast terminus of the Florida Trail in the Apalachicola National Forest. Head northwest from US 319 and traverse a lightly walked section of the Florida Trail, walking mostly on footpaths in rolling pine woods, coming to a lush woodland with old growth magnolias and other trees. Drop down to the Sopchoppy River valley and enjoy some of the best of the Florida Trail. Here the path meanders beneath live oaks alongside the blackwater stream, where huge cypress trees with oddly shaped knees line the waterway. Side streams cut deep gullies, making for a lot of ups and downs, though many of them are now bridged. Emerge onto a forest road and shortly come to Bradwell Bay Wilderness.

Start this segment of the Florida Trail by leaving US 319 behind, passing a trail register, and immediately entering an eye-pleasing forest of pine, live oak, and laurel oak. At 0.3 mile, come to a long and winding boardwalk over a low area of bay, titi, and cypress. Continue on a footpath in a more open forest. Come alongside and then cross Forest Road 356 at 1.0 mile. Drop down off a hill, nearing a thicket before turning back toward the forest road.

At mile 1.4 come to a longleaf plantation, dropping down to a titi thicket. The next thicket, with a wide stream beneath the dark canopy, is crossed at mile 1.9 on a plank bridge. Turn right and walk the margin dividing the pine woods from the stream just crossed. The land here consists of low sand hills of pine and turkey oak broken by titi thickets. Occasionally the trail takes forest roads for short sections. The faint footbed testifies to the infrequent use of the trail.

Step over a blackwater stream at mile 4.1. Turn left immediately past this crossing into a dense young longleaf plantation, cross a jeep track, and enter taller pines. At mile 5.1, come to a turkey oak stand atop a hill. Drop down to cross FR 321 at mile 5.3. The next section makes a lot of twists and turns—pay close attention here. First, cross FR 321C at mile 5.4, staying in thick woods, soon to pass under a power line.

Come back to FR 321C to span a stream on a low-water bridge. Immediately past the bridge, enter the forest to the right and settle back down to woods hiking. Pass through a pine plantation before coming to a mature pineland at mile 6.6. This area is favored by red-cockaded woodpeckers, as is evidenced by numerous pines circled with white paint stripes, marking trees with woodpecker nest holes.

At mile 7.2 come to an area with many live oaks and laurel oaks, with a brushy understory. This leads into the low area with many big trees. The trail can be mucky here. Of special note are the old growth sweetbay magnolia trees. Commonly known as bay trees or swamp magnolias, these trees keep their leaves year-round. They extend from South Florida northward to Massachusetts and westward to Texas. Look around for other large trees, such as red maple and tulip poplars. Stay in lush woods, mostly deciduous trees, before coming to one last section of big magnolias, then intersect FR 365 at mile 8.1. Cross the road and continue northwest through shady woods.

Drop to the banks of the Sopchoppy River and head upstream a short distance, coming to FR 346 at mile 8.5. Turn left on the sandy vehicle road and immediately span the Sopchoppy on a concrete bridge. The FT reenters the woods on the right along the west bank of the Sopchoppy River. This section of the Florida Trail was once known as the Apalachicola Trail.

A blue-blazed spur trail works around an old bridge upstream, but the Florida Trail keeps forward, crossing the same stream on a newer bridge. Immediately cross under a power line, then cross a small creek on a plank bridge at mile 9.1. Keep north through rich woods of water oak, sweetgum, red maple, and pine. Cross a feeder stream on a footbridge and swing around an inholding, coming to the banks of the Sop-choppy River at 9.4 miles. The trail is thirty feet above the river. Observe the huge cypress trees with their strange knees along the river. Soon you come to your first roller-coaster ride down then up a side stream gully. Most of the gullies flow only during rainy periods. The Florida Trail Association has been bridging many of these gullies.

At times the path turns away from the bluff instead of working around sharp bends in the Sopchoppy. The footbed can be narrow. Sand live oak, palmetto, live oak, and holly border the river and trail. Bluff heights range between twenty and fifty feet above the river. Continue to undulate, crossing cypress- and bamboo-filled ravines.

Leave the riverside at mile 10.1, passing through a titi-bay forest, and climb into pine flatwoods. Soon pick up a jeep track on high ground. Turkey oaks grow here. Veer right, away from the jeep track, at mile 10.8, and cross the new long-span bridge over Monkey Creek. The trail then rises up to a pine plantation and you walk among the rows of ever-greens.

Come to the riverbank at mile 11.2, once more enjoying the superlative beauty of the Sopchoppy River. And climb once more up and down the steep ravines, crossing a perennial feeder stream after 0.2 mile. Swamps occasionally appear; the trail effectively straddles the bluff between the Sopchoppy on the right and the overflow swamps on the left. At times the path drops right alongside the coffee-colored waters. Pass another perennial stream at mile 12.4. Soon the trail circumvents a wide swamp. Cross a series of boardwalk bridges before climbing to a dry open area, which is the official Sopchoppy River campsite. Past the camping area, pick up a wide trail that leads to FR 329. A bridge over the Sopchoppy is just to the right. The Florida Trail, however, turns left and follows FR 329 for 0.2 mile to the Bradwell Bay Wilderness trailhead, ending this segment. From here, it is 19.1 miles to Porter Lake.

Florida Trail, Bradwell Bay to Porter Lake

Begin: Bradwell Bay Wilderness trailhead at FR 329
End: Porter Lake Campground
Distance: 19.1 miles
Trail Difficulty: Potentially toughest hiking on the entire FT
Highlights: Federally designated wilderness, blackwater river
Hazards: Poorly marked mucky path, minimal trailbed, miles of swamp walking
Trail Connections: Florida Trail, Porter Lake to Vilas; Florida Trail, Medart to Bradwell Bay; Monkey Creek Connector Trail; FR 329 Connector Trail
Season: Fall–spring
Maps: Florida Trail Apalachicola East, Apalachicola National Forest map
Trailhead: To reach the east trailhead from the Wakulla Ranger Station on US 319 south of Tallahassee, head south on US 319 for 3.8 miles to Crawfordville and the Wakulla County Courthouse. Turn right at the stoplight just before the courthouse, on Arran Road (CR 368). Arran Road turns into Forest Highway 13. Follow Arran Road for 4.6 miles to FR 365. Turn left on FR 365 and follow it for 2.9 miles to FR 348. Turn right on FR 348 and follow it for 2.5 miles to FR 329. Turn left on FR 329 and follow it for 0.4 mile to the Bradwell Bay Wilderness trailhead, on your right.

To reach the east trailhead, Porter Lake Campground, from the junction of SR 263 and SR 20 west of Tallahassee, drive west on SR 20 for 17.5 miles to CR 375 (CR 375 turns into SR 375). Stay on 375 for 17.4 miles to Forest Highway 13. Turn right on FH 13 and follow it for 1.2 miles to Porter Lake Campground on your left. This section of the FT leaves from the campground itself.

This segment of the Florida Trail heads across the Bradwell Bay Wilderness and beyond to the banks of the Ochlockonee River. The wilderness is a land of contrasts, where the sun beats down over scant pines standing among palmetto prairies. Suddenly it enters miles of wet, shady cypress and hardwood swamps with little dry land, the toughest and most remote trail traveling in Florida's national forests. The trail then emerges into an area of dead pines ravaged by wildfire. Beyond the wilderness the path remains wet, cruising through row-cropped slash pines. Finally a little roadwalking is necessary, passing over the wide floodplain swamp surrounding the Ochlockonee River, to end at Porter Lake Campground.

Leave the Bradwell Bay parking area and enter the nearly 25,000-acre Bradwell Bay Wilderness, the largest wilderness in the Florida portion of the national forest system. This wide, wet depression was named for a hunter who was lost for days in the swamps and thickets of the area. After passing through the wilderness in its entirety, you will be appreciative of the orange blazes that mark the Florida Trail here.

Trace an old road, flanked by a canal, through mixed flatwoods of pine, sand live oak, and water oak. Pass a trail registration kiosk, then bridge a small creek surrounded by bamboo. Open into a sun-splashed brush plain, coming to pine woods at 0.8 mile. This wilderness is home to black bears—you may see their acorn-laden scat on the path. Black bears have made a serious comeback in the Apalachicola and other forests and preserves of the state.

Easily span a second creek on the remnants of a road bridge at mile 1.2. The trailside here is a mixed forest of oaks and pines. Enter a palmetto-gallberry plain over which the blackened trunks of burned pines tower. Ponds border the trail. Come to a stand of live oaks on trail left, which serve as a potential camping area, though water is not directly nearby. Also notice the increase in turkey oaks. Just a short distance past the live oaks, at 2.4 miles, leave the roadbed and make an acute turn left onto another less obvious roadbed. This left turn is signed. The roadbed you have been following continues north and becomes an unmaintained trail kept open by hunters and game.

Spindly pines crowd the path, giving way to a brush field stark with standing dead trees. The trailbed here is likely to be crowded with titi and wet in places. Wilderness trails are given less maintenance by design, to make the experience more challenging and rustic. Expect thick brush and fallen trees throughout Bradwell Bay Wilderness. Pond pines border the sloping ground next to the titi and in grow saucerlike depressions in the ragged prairies. Finding a campsite here can be difficult.

Come to a titi thicket in which is a six-foot-wide stream that must be crossed without a bridge. Cross a pine island and shortly come to a titi-bay-cypress thicket. Open onto a brush plain sparsely wooded in pine. Quickly bisect another titi thicket and continue on wet trail bordered in pond pine, more evidence of a high water table.

Figure 20. Johnny Molloy crosses a palmetto-gallberry plain in Bradwell Bay Wilderness. Photo by Johnny Molloy

Swing to the south around a saucer-shaped depression to your left at 4.1 miles, and enter a huge palmetto prairie. Orange-tipped metal poles indicate the trail. Also watch the footbed below for assurances that you are on the path. After a half mile a few trees begin to appear trailside, but the terrain is open more often than not. Pass a small pond to your right. Briefly traverse another bay thicket with a small stream running through it before coming to a trail junction in an open area at mile 5.2. To your left, a blue-blazed side trail leads 0.5 mile through palmetto prairie and turkey oaks to FR 329 at Monkey Creek.

The Florida Trail continues right, turning onto an old jeep road and entering pine flatwoods. Keep west in these woods and descend into a titi-cypress swamp, crossing a feeder stream of Monkey Creek at 6.2 miles. You can see bridge remnants in the water of this stream. Just before this feeder stream is a scrub live oak copse that is the best campsite for miles, level and shady and known as The Oaks. Emerge onto a palmetto plain with a few scattered pond and longleaf pines. The trail is brushy in spots.

Drop again to ford Monkey Creek at mile 7.1. By now you have given up hope of keeping your boots dry. Stay in a lush shady woodland on the far side of Monkey Creek. This lush forest gives way to tall longleaf woodland. Watch here as the trail unexpectedly turns sharply right and passes through a swamp. Climb back to pine woods, the last significant dry ground for over a mile and a half, and intersect to a blue-blazed side trail at mile 7.7. It leads left 150 yards to FR 329.

Descend into a wet area of bay, pond pine, and cypress. This swamp section is broken by one little area of pines three quarters of a mile distant. Before the water is finished dribbling off your legs atop this little pine island from the swamp just crossed, enter another swamp that goes unbroken a long while. Look into the water around you and look for flow of the swamp—the water flows against you. Emerge onto a larger pine island, Bradwell Island, at mile 9.0. This area was burned and has many standing dead trees. Savor the dry ground here and realize that this provides the last viable camping area for miles.

Leaving Bradwell Island, you enter a long swamp. Above are old growth trees—pine, cypress, and gum. Look for a huge double-trunked

Figure 21. Johnny Molloy swamp slogging in a muddy section of Bradwell Bay Wilderness. Photo By Johnny Molloy

cypress on trail left at mile 9.6. At mile 9.9, the still waters can be mucky in area of deciduous swamp trees. It has more open sections of water that can reach above your knees. Roots, submerged logs, and deep pockets make for uneven and rough going. This is where the biggest trees are, too. Be very careful, and have the most critical items in your pack waterproofed. In times of high water, you will be submerged to your waist.

By mile 10.5 the water becomes shallower, but the footing is still very uneven. There are scattered places to rest or sit down. Enter an area where the swamp hardwoods are thin. Pass through one more deep section before emerging onto dry land and picking up a logging tram berm with canals on both sides. The dry land is open. Turn once again into swamp, still tracing the tram bed. This swamp tromp is brief. Climb out to a pine forest, where most of the trees are living and the trail is mostly dry. But parts of the area have been burned, and some trail sections are wet. Follow the old tram road, crossing more titi thicket and taking one last wet-footed wilderness walk before coming to FR 314 at 12.3 miles.

Leave the Bradwell Bay Wilderness at FR 314. Turn right and walk along the forest road for 0.6 mile, passing a beekeeper's hive on your left. Leave the forest road and turn left onto a four-wheel-drive track through a pine plantation with canals cut along it. The water table is quite high here, and the path can be wet. Come to a titi-cypress thicket and plunge into the water. There is just enough high ground around to attempt to keep your feet dry, but sooner or later they are going to get wet. Leave the titi thicket and come to a pine plantation. This wet area was row-cropped—rows were dug and the slash pines were planted on the higher ground between the rows in pursuit of better growing conditions. For the hiker it means wet feet even though the trail passes through a pine plantation, which normally means dry walking.

At mile 13.8 come to an unnumbered but sporadically maintained forest road. Follow this road forward to FR 388 at mile 14.1. Turn right on FR 388 and follow it for 0.6 mile to double orange blazes. Leave the forest road left and enter another wet pine plantation on an ultra-rough four-wheel-drive track. Brush such as yaupon lines the path. Pass through a pine-titi-bay thicket on a side trail, avoiding deep water on the jeep road. At mile 15.2 the trail sidetracks again in a titi-cypress thicket. A blackwater creek, Flat Branch, flows through the center of this thicket.

Backpackers have camped on the west side of this stream in the past, including me.

Stay the course westerly, making detours only around muddy water on the jeep track. Emerge onto SR 375 at 16.0 miles. The Florida Trail turns right and follows the paved road north over Smith Creek. However, just to the left is the Langston Homestead. Look across road for blue blazes leading along Allen Lake Road, then left through woods to reach the wooden house with a tin roof. The place is shaded by huge live oaks but is in disrepair. A trail leads behind the house to a wooden-boxed spring that will likely need cleaning out. I hope the Langston Homestead will be restored as a historic interpretive area.

The FT leaves SR 375 at mile 16.9, veering left onto private land for 0.9 mile. This portion of the trail is for Florida Trail Association members only. It picks up an old roadbed then spans a clear branch and passes along a richly wooded bluff line, where magnolias and beech trees thrive. The trail then emerges on FH 13 to span the Ochlockonee River and reach Porter Lake Campground at 19.1 miles.

If you are not a Florida Trail member, stay on SR 375 for 0.5 mile to FH 13. Turn left on FH 13, and follow it for 1.2 miles until the Florida Trail emerges onto FH 13, just before the bridge over the Ochlockonee River. Span the Ochlockonee on the bridge and proceed, passing another bridge over Porter Lake, and drop off the road after 0.6 mile to Porter Lake Campground, ending this segment of the Florida Trail at mile 19.1. From here it is 18.4 miles northwest to Vilas on the Florida Trail.

Florida Trail, Porter Lake to Vilas

Begin: Porter Lake campground
End: Vilas trailhead at State Road 65
Distance: 18.4 miles
Trail Difficulty: Moderate
Highlights: Numerous streams, wiregrass prairies, former turpentining community
Hazards: Wobbly footbridges
Trail Connections: Florida Trail, Vilas to Camel Lake; Florida Trail, Bradwell Bay to Porter Lake
Season: Fall–spring
Maps: Florida Trail Apalachicola West, Apalachicola National Forest map
Trailhead: To reach the east trailhead, Porter Lake Campground, from junction of SR 263 and SR 20 west of Tallahassee, drive west on SR 20 for 17.5 miles to CR 375 (CR 375 turns into SR 375). Stay on 375 for 17.4 miles to FH 13. Turn right on FH 13 and follow it for 1.2 miles to Porter Lake Campground on your left. This section of the FT leaves from the campground.

To reach the west terminus of the trail, Vilas, from the Apalachicola Ranger Station in Bristol, head west on SR 20 for 0.4 mile to SR 12. Turn left on SR 12 and follow it for 13 miles south to FR 108. Turn left on FR 108 and follow it 3 miles to FR 112. Turn right on FR 112 and follow it 4.5 miles to SR 65. Turn left on SR 65 and follow it 0.4 mile to FR 120. Turn right on FR 120 and follow it 0.2 mile to the trailhead on the left just after the railroad tracks.

This segment of the Florida Trail is ideal for backpacking. The pathway heads west from Porter Lake, crossing numerous streams, sometimes on footbridges and sometimes on road bridges. A variety of environments lie along the way. Pine palmetto flatwoods give way to titi, cypress, and hardwoods along streams and swamps. Extensive prairies of wiregrass, dotted with longleaf pine, lie in the middle of this section. Camping possibilities are scattered alongside the trail. Expect to have little company, and that includes while walking forest roads during the week or in nonhunting periods.

Leave Porter Lake Campground heading west in a thick woodland of water oak, magnolia, and loblolly pine, and crossing a swamp on a long footlog at 0.2 mile. Keep along the path and cross FH 13 at 0.7 mile. Turn northerly in a longleaf pine woodland, picking up a jeep trail. Cross a small branch at 0.9 mile on a footlog. The path climbs a bit and enters a young pine plantation. Leave the jeep trail. Straddle the perimeter between longleaf on your left and a floodplain marsh on your right.

Span another stream on a footlog. Emerge into a longleaf-wiregrass-palmetto woodland, paralleling the stream just crossed. In an open field, the trail veers off to the right. Cross another stream on a footlog at 2.1 miles. Climb into a slash pine plantation. Keep up with the orange blazes as the Florida Trail changes jeep tracks frequently. This area is laced not only with jeep trails but also with wet titi thickets and small creeks, which is why the FT follows jeep tracks here—they are often the highest places around.

But the FT is primarily a footpath, as is evidenced by the next section that heads through tulip trees, water oaks, and bay trees with a lot of cane, too. At 2.9 miles, cross FR 142, spanning Hickory Branch, then veer left into longleaf woodland. Drop steeply off a turkey oak hill to cross Coxes Branch on a log bridge at mile 4.3. The old suspension bridge has been dismantled. Notice the large loblolly pines here. Loblolly pines prefer deep, poorly drained floodplains in the Apalachicola. The word *loblolly* is Creek Indian for mud puddle. But this southeastern pine also grows in fertile uplands and old fields.

Keep in a titi-cane thicket, now paralleling Indian Creek. Cross paved County Road 67 at 4.5 miles. Turn right on the road, spanning Indian Creek, then turn left into a hilly area that becomes grown over with turkey oaks, then longleaf. Pick up a jeep trail at 5.2 miles and keep west, reaching FR 177 at mile 5.6.

Stay in turkey oak-longleaf-wiregrass, dropping to a wet area of pond pine and cypress, before coming to FR 107 at mile 6.5. Make a westerly road walk on this forest road that is the only dry footing for miles—the water table is just below ground level. Cross the headwaters of Indian Creek, coming to the junction with FR 126 at 7.2 miles. Stay forward on FR 107. Pine plantations growing over soaked brush flank the road.

At mile 8.7, on a curve, dive left into thick brush and pine. The woods become increasingly wet, with titi thickets along a creek. The trail is often blazed with paint, and orange blocks of wood have been nailed to trees. Stay in the brush, crossing a floodplain and stream on a long plank bridge just before crossing FR 175 at 9.8 miles.

The Florida Trail continues forward alongside the headwaters of Bay Creek, meandering in the margin between wet and dry woods. Cross Bay Creek at 11.6 miles. Span a log-choked creek or old canal with the aid of steel cables at Bay Creek at 12.0 miles. Emerge into an impressive a prairie of wiregrass, dotted with longleaf pines. There are good views into the forest beyond. The FT turns sharply right, now as a foot trail, and borders the perimeter of the prairie. A titi thicket lies to your right. Pond pines grow where the wiregrass and titi come together. Leave the longleaf prairie, dropping into a floodplain swamp, crossing a black-water stream and beginning a pattern of alternating between wiregrass prairies and floodplain swamps. This area oozes solitude, even with the crossing of FR 107B at mile 13.6.

Keep with the wiregrass-swamp pattern, and bisect Saplin Head Swamp at 15.4 miles. This entails crossing a long, nasty titi thicket. Turn north in wiregrass topped with longleaf and turkey oaks, coming to Forest Road 107 at mile 16.2 miles. Turn left on FR 107, and span Black Creek on a road bridge. Look for Atlantic white cedar along the fringes of the watercourse. Cross a tributary stream of Black Creek at mile 16.9, then head north on a foot trail, paralleling the feeder stream. Turn away from the feeder stream and dip down through a few titi-bay thickets between pinelands.

At mile 18.2, come to the Vilas campsite, on your right beneath tall pines. Beyond this is the former community of Vilas, which was based on turpentining. Its prime was from the 1920s through the 1940s. Look around for relics of that era, but leave them for others to enjoy. The Florida naval stores industry actually began in 1743 at Pensacola with the shipment of pine pitch, turpentine, and pine logs on a schooner bound for Havana. The nearest water is at the New River, south of where the Florida Trail emerges onto SR 65. Filtering is recommended.

Come to FR 120 and end this segment of the Florida Trail at mile 18.4. From here it is 10.0 miles to Camel Lake campground, and 15.3 miles to SR 12 and the end of the Florida Trail through the Apalachicola National Forest at Estiffanulga.

Florida Trail, Vilas to Estiffanulga

Begin: Vilas trailhead at State Road 65
End: SR 12 near Estiffanulga
Distance: 15.3 miles
Trail Difficulty: Moderate to difficult
Highlights: Memery Island, numerous creeks, lakes, and savannas
Hazards: Sun, swamps
Trail Connections: Florida Trail, Porter Lake to Vilas; Trail of Lakes Loop;
Camel Lake Loop
Season: Fall–spring
Maps: Florida Trail Apalachicola West, Apalachicola National Forest map
Trailhead: To reach the east terminus of the trail from the Apalachicola
Ranger Station in Bristol, head west on SR 20 for 0.4 mile to SR 12. Turn left
on SR 12 and follow it for 13 miles to FR 108. Turn left on FR 108 and follow
it 3 miles to FR 112. Turn right on FR 112 and follow it 4.5 miles to SR 65.
Turn left on SR 65 and follow it 0.4 mile to FR 120. Turn right on FR 120 and
follow it 0.2 mile to the trailhead on the left just after the railroad tracks.

To reach the west terminus of the trail from the Apalachicola Ranger
Station in Bristol, head west on SR 20 for 0.4 mile to SR 12. Turn left on SR
12 and follow it for 10 miles to the Florida Trail, which exits the forest on
the left side of the road.

This hike traverses numerous environments and additionally offers vertical variation. Leave Vilas and pass along the floodplain of the New River. Past here the trailbed can be wet, passing through a full-scale swamp. Climb to higher, drier ground and reach pretty Bonnet Pond, ringed in cypress, and the Trail of Lakes Loop. Head through turkey oaks, then cross the perennial stream Big Gully Creek and the cool swamp woods around it. Pass over dry hills and down into a juniper swamp, then on to crystal-clear Camel Lake, a national forest recreation area and campground. Past Camel Lake, climb Memery Island, a sandy knob topped in live oaks. Finally, enjoy unique savannas—grassy wetlands pocked with pine, where carnivorous pitcher plants thrive among widely scattered pines. Numerous potential camping spots make this section ideal for backpackers.

Figure 22. Sandra Friend kneels by blooming pitcher plants. Photo by Rob Smith Jr.

Leave Vilas, heading west on Forest Road 120 just a short distance over the Apalachicola Northern railroad tracks, and turn left into a tall wood with a marshy footbed. At 0.3 mile, come to SR 65 and turn left again, crossing the New River on a road bridge. At 0.7 mile come to FR 112 and turn right, tracing the sandy road just a short distance before heading right again, through an ATV-proof fence, paralleling the floodplain swamp of the New River in young longleaf growth. Notice the Atlantic white cedars on the swamp edge. They become common on the streams west of here.

At mile 1.8 drop down along the New River on a wet trail shadowed by tall cypress. When leaving the swamp, look for carnivorous pitcher plants in the trailside grass before climbing to a pine plantation with a brushy understory. The trail jumps on and off an old forest road before reaching FR 112H at 3.2 miles. Turn right here and cross Hostage Branch on the road bridge. Veer left onto a foot trail that passes through brushy woods with a wet footbed in many spots. Drop into the swamp of Shuler Bay at mile 4.3. A boardwalk extends for a half mile.

At mile 5.6, enter private land—the property boundary is marked. Pass through the private land for 0.3 mile and return to national forest land, now on little-used FR 108D. Turkey oaks increase in number. Pass a large field on your right just before crossing FR 108 at mile 6.2. Ahead the forest road splits—take the right fork and follow FR 108E briefly, before the trail splits right away from the road, paralleling a titi thicket.

At 6.6 miles, cross FR 108 and reach a trail junction. The south terminus of the Trail of Lakes comes in from the right. Dead ahead is Bonnet Pond. The shore makes a good camping locale. Stay left on the FT and along the shore of Bonnet Pond. Check out the widely buttressed cypress trees that encircle the small body of water. Pass by another smaller pond before turning away from the water, alongside a wet strand to your left. Circle a normally dry lake bed to your left at mile 7.7, then pick up a straight dug path, which was a fire break at one time. Drop off the hill and come to FR 105 at mile 8.2. Turn left along the forest road and bridge Big Gully Creek. Past the creek, leave the road and turn left again, climbing a hilltop.

Cruise along the hilltop toward Camel Lake, through turkey oak and sand live oak. Drop into a thicket at mile 9.0, crossing an unnamed stream on a plank bridge. Continue walking the plank until the trail emerges into a well-drained pine-oak woodland, soon coming to another plank bridge through a juniper-filled swamp strand. At mile 10.0, reach the side trail leading left to Camel Lake. Potable water can be obtained from the campground spigots. The revamped campground has a campground host and makes for good long-term parking if you are going to hike the FT through the Apalachicola. There is currently no parking on SR 12.

The FT leaves Camel Lake and crosses Forest Road 105. Continue north in longleaf–turkey oak. Abruptly turn right and cross a small creek on another plank bridge. Beyond this are interpretive signs identifying prevalent trees of the forest. Parallel a stream, then dive left into a titi thicket, emerging back to a wetland of bay, grass, and pine. The full name for bay is sweetbay magnolia. It grows primarily in wet areas. Its thick green leaves, with a silvery underside, are evident from afar on a windy day.

Leave the low wet area and climb a hill to pick up a jeep track at 10.8 mile. Drop down to yet another wet area of bay, Atlantic white cedar, and cypress. Atlantic white cedar is an interesting tree. It is a tall evergreen with a spirelike crown and slender branches, and grows in a belt fifty to a hundred miles wide along the coastline from Maine to Mississippi. This evergreen likes to grow in wet swampy areas and alongside cool, clear waterways. During the Revolutionary War the wood of this tree was made into charcoal for gunpowder.

Stay alongside a wet area to your left, called Johnson Juniper Swamp, looking for more Atlantic white cedars—the trail is in turkey oaks and pine. Part of this area has been timbered. Come to a trail junction at 12.0 miles. To your right, the blue-blazed Trail of Lakes leaves right and heads south to connect to the FT near Bonnet Lake. The orange-blazed Florida Trail turns left and enters a titi thicket. Keep along a cool, shady elevated jeep trail that bisects Johnson Juniper Swamp. Climb out of the thicket onto Memery Island—an island of rich soil encircled by titi thickets and poorer, sandy soils. On top of the Memery are live oak, laurel oak, and magnolia. Top out on the island at mile 12.1. Drop down again and cross a small creek, as the FT works around mud holes in the jeep trail.

At mile 12.7, leave the jeep trail. Beyond this, savannas begin. These savannas are mostly grass but have scattered longleaf pine and cypress. Submerged during wetter times of the year, and fire prone during drier times, these savannas harbor unique flora such as the pitcher plant, which traps insects and ingests them. Butterworts and sundews are other carnivores. Wildflowers are abundant here during the spring. The trailbed of thick grass is apt to be wet and clumpy. A swamp strand interrupts the savanna at mile 12.8. The grassy plains offer long views. At mile 13.7 cross another swamp strand, but soon return to the savanna, coming to FR 150 at mile 14.2.

Turn right on FR 150, spanning Little Gully Creek to turn right on a little-used often muddy jeep trail. Leave the jeep trail at mile 14.5, veering left on a footpath into a tall longleaf forest. The path is well blazed here, though the trailbed is indistinct. Open into a savanna. Off to your right is private land planted thickly in pines. Bisect a cypress slough before walking through one last savanna and coming to State Road 12 at Estiffanulga at 15.3 miles. This is the end of the FT in the Apalachicola National Forest.

Camel Lake Loop

Begin: Camel Lake Recreation Area
End: Camel Lake Recreation Area
Distance: 1.2-mile loop
Trail Difficulty: Easy
Highlights: Views of Camel Pond
Hazards: Poison ivy
Trail Connections: Florida Trail, Trail of Lakes Loop
Season: Year-round
Maps: None
Trailhead: Follow CR 12 south from the CR 12 and SR 20 intersection in Bristol into the Apalachicola National Forest. Shortly after you pass the regional work center on the left, watch for FR 105. A small sign directs you to Camel Lake Recreation Area. Follow the road for 2 miles and then turn right and park inside Camel Lake Recreation Area. A $3 per vehicle fee applies. The recreation area is open daily from 8:00 a.m. to 8:00 p.m. April 1–October 31, 8:00 a.m. to 6:00 p.m. November 1–March 31.

From the restrooms nearest the parking area, walk down toward the lake to the right. Follow an old jeep road to reach the boat ramp parking area (an alternate parking spot), where you'll see the first hiker symbol sign. Blue blazes lead you down this broad trail, wide enough for two to walk together, which circles around Camel Pond. It is not a lake, despite the name of the recreation area, but a crystal-clear pond where wax myrtle lines the shore. Enjoy great views from the southern shore as you walk beneath a canopy of tall longleaf pine and turkey oaks. You pass numbered marker 3 after 0.5 mile. This and other markers are reminders of points of interest that were once described in an interpretive brochure, no longer available at the recreation area. Soon after stepping over a downed tree, you reach the back of a hiker symbol sign. The trail turns left to parallel the lake; a side trail to Little Camel Pond has been abandoned.

After you pass marker 6, a double blue blaze directs you right along a mild curve, following the lakeshore. Marker 7 is 0.9 mile around the loop, where the pines and turkey oaks offer a fair amount of shade. The trail parallels the campground briefly before reaching a double blaze and the edge of the grassy open space along the lake at 1.1 miles. Continue straight across the open space to return to the parking area, finishing at 1.2 miles. Alternatively, you can turn right at the double blaze and make a beeline across the campground entrance to reach the Florida Trail near where it crosses FR 105; this is also the access point for the Trail of Lakes Loop.

Fort Gadsden Trail

Begin: Fort Gadsden parking area
End: Fort Gadsden parking area
Distance: 0.9-mile loop
Trail Difficulty: Easy
Highlights: Historic site, views of Apalachicola River
Hazards: Area is prone to flooding; if there is water across the entrance road, the historic site is flooded and you should turn back
Trail Connections: None
Season: Fall–spring
Maps: Sometimes available in the information box on site
Trailhead: From SR 65 south of Sumatra, turn right onto Brickyard Road at the Fort Gadsden sign and drive 1.9 miles. This is an unpaved road that can be very bumpy. Turn left onto Fort Gadsden Road and continue 1 mile to the park entrance. Follow the road around to the parking area.

Start your hike at the parking area, where a trail leads past a picnic shelter and up to a historic marker. Peek in the information box for an interpretive guide to this historic site. Built in 1814 to encourage Seminoles to ally with the British, the first fort was abandoned and later occupied by free blacks who rallied for the British cause in Spanish Florida. The path skirts a shelter with exhibits further deepening your knowledge of local history. Swinging toward a line of cypress trees along the Apalachicola River, the trail crosses a short bridge and passes a sign indicating "British Fort North Moat." Two different forts sat on this site: the initial British fort and Fort Gadsden, built in 1818 and occupied through the Civil War. Walk past the bits and pieces of 1838 steamship boilers and up to the flagpole, where a bench provides a scenic spot to survey the swiftly flowing Apalachicola River and the former site of Fort Gadsden.

From here the trail is not distinct but is easy to find: from the bench, look past the flagpole to a breach in a small levee around the fort site. You'll spy a British flag flying from another flagpole in the distance. Head for it. Known as the "Negro Fort," this small fortress was a thorn in the side of Andrew Jackson, who saw its potential for stopping commerce along the Apalachicola River. On the morning of July 27, 1816, a

U.S. naval vessel commanded by Duncan Clinch fired a single shot that exploded the powder magazine at this site, killing 270 of the fort's 300 occupants.

Follow the arrow sign on the far side of the clearing to a footpath into the forest. Stately pines rise overhead. The path leads you into a clearing marked as the Renegade Cemetery, where the victims of the 1816 blast are buried. At the far edge of this clearing is the hand-lettered wooden sign "Wiregrass-Gentian Trail," at 0.5 mile. Follow this pleasant path through the wiregrass under the pines, where delicate endangered wiregrass gentian shows its white blooms in late fall and winter. At the end of the trail you reach the entrance road. Turn left and follow the entrance road berm back to the parking area to complete a loop of 0.9 mile.

Gum Swamp Trail

Begin: Leon Sinks Geological Area
End: Leon Sinks Geological Area
Distance: 2.6-mile loop
Trail Difficulty: Easy
Highlights: Scenic swamps
Hazards: Mosquitoes, poison ivy
Trail Connections: Crossover Trail, Sinkhole Trail
Season: Fall–spring
Maps: Available at trailhead
Trailhead: From the junction of SR 61 and US 319 just south of Tallahassee, head south on US 319 for 4 miles to the Leon Sinks Geological Area, on your right. The trailhead kiosk adjoins the restrooms.

Complementing the Sinkhole Trail, the Gum Swamp Trail provides a look at the swamps along the lowlands just south of the hilly karst at Leon Sinks Geological Area. It's an excellent place to enjoy fragrant native azalea in the spring. While you can hike either of the loops separately, if you choose to hike the Sinkhole Trail and Gum Swamp Trail together, they form a 4-mile outer loop to the trail system.

Start your hike at the trailhead kiosk. At the trail junction, turn left. Follow the lime green blazes through the sand hills to a trail junction at 0.2 mile. Turn left to explore the spur trail to Gopher Hole, a cave that looks like a giant gopher tortoise burrow. The spur trail ends at a stone lip looking into the watery cave. Backtrack to the main trail and turn left. Continue to the Crossover Trail sign, and go straight. The Crossover Trail leads you on a boardwalk through the Gum Swamp and meets the Sinkhole Trail at 0.8 mile. Turn left and follow the Gum Swamp Trail past an interesting rock formation along Fisher Creek. The trail heads into mixed pines and uplands.

You'll find Florida azalea in bloom each spring along the next half mile of trail. Pine cones cover the forest floor, and the footpath is on a nice layer of pine duff. The trail veers right; to the left is a depression in the distance, the gum swamp you walked through on the Crossover Trail. Pass a marker with a lime green arrow at 1.4 miles before the trail crosses an old jeep track. The forest becomes denser, with large loblolly pines and longleaf pines.

You reach scenic Bear Scratch Swamp after a bench at 1.6 miles. It's a beauty spot—take the time to sit and watch for waterfowl and wildlife. At South Swamp, look for a pine and water oak that have grown intertwined, right near the sign. The next swamp is Shadows Swamp, at 2.1 miles.

You reach the Crossover Trail again at 2.3 miles. Turn right this time to exit, passing the spur trail to Gopher Hole before you return to the first trail junction. Turn right to exit to the parking area.

Silver Lake Habitat Trail

Begin: Silver Lake
End: Silver Lake
Distance: 1.2-mile loop
Trail Difficulty: Easy
Highlights: Great views of Silver Lake, nice boardwalk
Hazards: Skirts close to prime alligator habitat
Trail Connections: None
Season: Year-round
Maps: None
Trailhead: From the intersection of SR 263 (Capital Circle West) and SR 20, drive west on SR 20 for 3.6 miles to Silver Lake Road, between two convenience stores on the left. Turn left and follow the road 3.1 miles to the entrance on the left. There is a $3 per car day use fee at the entrance gate. Drive down to the far parking area and park near the large building, which is the restroom. The recreation area is open daily from 8:00 a.m. to 8:00 p.m. April 1–October 31, 8:00 a.m. to 6:00 p.m. November 1–March 31.

This short trail loops around Silver Lake, showcasing the habitats along the lake. Start your hike by parking near the restrooms in the main parking area and walk down toward the lakeshore. Follow the lakeshore to the left to find the "Silver Lake Habitat Trail" sign at a boardwalk. Turn right at the blue blaze and walk down the boardwalk, which provides views across and into the crystal-clear water. As you leave the boardwalk, the trail makes an abrupt right turn and follows the lake closely. The next interpretive sign is about how the lake formed, with a nice view of the lake behind it. You will see many interpretive signs along this journey. At a junction with a jeep road, turn right. Cross over a launch point for canoes and kayaks. You reach a bench at 0.4 mile, from which you can see straight across the lake to the swimming area.

As you walk, the footpath meanders through upland forests of hardwoods and pine flatwoods, with an understory of oaks, as well as through a climax laurel oak forest. These tall trees start falling down in chunks once they reach the age of about seventy years. In early spring there are

Florida dogwoods in bloom, and later in the spring, you'll note the sweet scent of southern magnolia blossoms. Large pine cones draw your attention to the longleaf pines shading the footpath. Passing the "Longleaf pines and fire" interpretive marker, the trail swings left to follow an arm of Silver Lake where cypresses line the shore. You pass a pine with deep scars from turpentine tapping.

At 0.7 mile a blue blaze directs you right onto a path coming from the left that reaches a clearing along the shoreline. The pitch of the land becomes more steeply sloped down to the lake as you walk under large magnolias. The trail continues uphill and swings right to become a broad path heading in a straight line toward a gap in a fence. At 1 mile, you pass through the gap and emerge into the picnic area, passing an abandoned amphitheatre on the right. The blazes end here. Walk across the picnic area under the oaks to reach the parking area and complete the 1.2-mile loop.

Sinkhole Trail

Begin: Leon Sinks Geological Area
End: Leon Sinks Geological Area
Distance: 3-mile loop
Trail Difficulty: Moderate
Highlights: Deep sinkholes and hilly terrain
Hazards: Steep dropoffs, poison ivy
Trail Connections: Crossover Trail, Gum Swamp Trail
Season: Fall–spring
Maps: Available at trailhead
Trailhead: From the junction of SR 61 and US 319 just south of Tallahassee, head south on US 319 for 4 miles to the Leon Sinks Geological Area, on your right. The trailhead kiosk adjoins the restrooms.

The Leon Sinks Geological Area offers a unique look into Florida's karst topography. The Woodville Karst Plain contains an aquifer with interconnected passageways that run from the Tallahassee area down toward St. Marks. Intrepid cave divers have mapped some of the passageways, while others have been discovered by dropping dye into sinkholes to see where it emerges in springs. Of the two major trails in this geological area, the Sinkhole Trail focuses on showcasing karst features.

Start your hike at the trailhead kiosk. At the trail junction, turn right and follow the blue blazes into the sand hills. The trail heads down a flight of stairs into Dry Sink, a depression filled with dogwood and magnolia. Rise up and loop around deep Turner Sink, with a bench overlook. Crossing an old track at 0.3 mile, you circle the left side of Cone Sink and pass Palmetto Sink, reaching Back Sink at 0.4 mile. A side trail leads down into the sink and passes by its two throatlike bowls at the bottom.

Far Sink is on the right at 0.5 mile. As you continue along a ridge, you see an aqua pool below—Hammock Sink. Enjoy this picturesque water-filled sink from a boardwalk and observation platform.

Next you encounter Tiny Sink, then rise up into the open sand hills to discover Big Dismal Sink, which at 130 feet is the deepest sink in the Woodville Karst Plain. You can hear water dripping from the fern-

Figure 23. A boardwalk and platform lead to Hammock Sink. Photo by Sandra Friend

draped rimrock into this karst window. The trail continues past Field Sink and then enters a shady upland at 1.2 miles, headed straight for Big Eight Sink—don't plunge in! Next is Magnolia Sink with its odd rock formations. Pass Black Sink and a bench, then the trail crosses a couple of old jeep tracks before heading into shadier uplands.

Past the clearing with benches, you have your choice of following the high water route or heading downhill to see Duckweed Sink and the bridge over Lost Stream Sink. Climb back up the steps to main trail and turn left. You reach the junction with the Crossover Trail and Gum Swamp Trail at 2.1 mile at the Natural Bridge, where Fisher Creek (the "Lost Stream") rises as a spring and flows away past a large rock formation. Go straight ahead on the Crossover Trail, which leads you on a boardwalk through a gum swamp. At mile 2.6, meet the Gum Swamp Trail at the other side of the swamp and continue straight, past the side trail to Gopher Hole, to return to the first trail junction. Turn right to exit to the parking area.

Trail of Lakes Loop

Begin: Camel Lake Recreation Area
End: Camel Lake Recreation Area
Distance: 9.5-mile loop
Trail Difficulty: Moderate
Highlights: Pitcher plant prairies, scenic views
Hazards: Poison ivy, mucky lowlands
Trail Connections: Florida Trail, Vilas to Estiffanulga
Season: Fall–spring
Maps: Florida Trail Apalachicola West
Trailhead: Follow CR 12 south from the CR 12 and SR 20 intersection in Bristol for 11.4 miles into the Apalachicola National Forest. Shortly after you pass the regional work center on the left, watch for FR 105. A small sign directs you to Camel Lake Recreation Area. Follow the road for 2 miles and then turn right and park inside Camel Lake Recreation Area. A $3 per vehicle fee applies. The recreation area is open daily 8:00 a.m. to 8:00 p.m. April 1–October 31, and 8:00 a.m. to 6:00 p.m. November 1–March 31. If you wish to start your hike earlier, park along FR 105 near the trail crossing.

The Trail of Lakes is a 3.9-mile blue-blazed connector between two portions of the Florida Trail around Camel Lake. To enjoy it as a day hike with no shuttling, you can use the Florida Trail to create a 9.5-mile loop through a variety of habitats.

Start your hike at the Camel Lake Recreation Area main parking area. Walk along FR 105 a short distance north to the Florida Trail crossing. Turn left to head northwest. After 0.2 mile, turn right at double blazes in front of a picnic table, crossing a plank bridge over a stream. The trail turns sharply left. Routed interpretive signs identify numerous trees along this portion of the trail. After 0.6 mile, a double blaze directs you onto a jeep road briefly; a young pine plantation is off to the right. The trail quickly veers off to the left. Watch for a double blaze leading you left down a shady tunnel into a pine plantation. You pass a pine tree that has swallowed a board.

At mile 0.8 the trail drops into a wet area beneath the shade of fra-

Figure 24. Titi blooms are tiny but grow in such profusion that they perfume large areas. Photo by Johnny Molloy

grant titi trees. It opens up into a pine savanna where hooded pitcher plants rise from seepage bogs, some right in the footpath. You reach the 1-mile mark when the trail rises into dry sand hills. Reach a jeep road at a T-junction and turn left. The trail drops down into a mucky wet corridor with cypress knees; it is hard to see the blazes here. Follow the tunnel to where it opens into pine flatwoods. The trail hugs the edge of the habitat. Turn left into another titi tunnel at 1.9 mile, and emerge back into open sand hills as the trail turns left.

At 2.1 miles, you reach the Trail of Lakes junction at a jeep road with a routed sign to the left. Turn right to follow the blue blazes up the jeep road at the base of the sand hills, passing two clearings on the right. At 2.6 miles you cross a forest road and enter a longleaf pine forest, where the high canopy shades an understory of saw palmetto. The trail skirts a dome of titi at 2.9 miles, and you can see a sand road off to the left. A distinct clearing with wheat-colored grasses—a small prairie pond, often dry—sits off to the left at 3.4 miles. You pass through a titi stand at 3.7 miles and emerge back into the longleaf pine forest.

At 4 miles the trail turns right at a double blaze into the sand hills, where turkey oaks wave their leaves in the breeze, and drops down to follow the ecotone between this habitat and the titi swamp. After 4.3 miles the trail crosses FR 136, where the blue blazes lead you onto a jeep trail. It then turns left into the shade of titi on a series of balance-beam-like plank bridges over a flowing stream, with no cable to assist your crossing. Plunging into deep shade, the footpath parallels the creek; be careful of cypress knees. Cross two high bridges with cable handrails at 4.5 miles as the trail snakes through a hummocky bottomland, flooded during the wet season. Climb up a rugged rooty slope into the sand hills.

Crossing a jeep trail, you can see a large body of water in the distance—Sheep Island Lake. The chorus of frogs grows louder as you reach a side trail to the lake at 4.7 miles. Walk down and enjoy the view of water lilies and the pristine far shoreline. The trail continues around the lake but out of sight of it. At 4.9 miles, turn left onto a jeep road and keep alert for a double blaze that leads you back into the woods on the left. A confusing array of double blazes in several directions greets you at the next intersection; just cross the intersection and look for the next blaze to confirm. The footpath passes under longleaf pines before dropping into a bottomland with a series of rotting plank bridges crossing streamlets. There is little shade overhead as you rise up into the sand hills again. Look for the blazes here on metal fenceposts.

A sinkhole sits off to the left as the trail rises up into a more mature forest. Cross FR 105 diagonally to the right. The trail immediately meets FR 108E. Turn left on this narrow sand road—do not cross the road to the more obvious footpath. It's tough to see the dark blue blazes on the darker oak bark, but they are there. After 5.7 miles you pass a clearing on the right for parking and see the outline of trees around Bonnet Pond, off to the right.

The Trail of Lakes ends at the Florida Trail at 6 miles, where you encounter another routed directional sign. Turn right and start following the orange blazes beneath the oaks and pines toward Bonnet Pond; the trail provides an excellent view of this cypress-lined jewel. Cross a jeep trail at 6.4 miles and enter a plantation of tall skinny pines. The habitat transitions to sand hills, with sand road to the right. At 7 miles, a small pond sits in a depression to the right. The trail parallels a titi-lined drainage. Passing a sand pit piled with cut trees and construction debris, the trail crosses a jeep road at 7.2 miles and then loops around the pit before making a sharp left into the sand hills. You continue down a long, straight stretch until the trail finally veers right at 7.6 miles.

Emerging onto a sand road, you'll turn left to follow it across a broad creek before you follow the blazes left and uphill into the sand hills—you won't miss the Florida Trail signs. Following a jeep road, the trail starts to parallel another titi-lined drainage at 8 miles, rising into a young pine forest. A double blaze leads you onto a jeep trail at 8.3 miles as the trail curves right into shade. The trail crosses a forest road and then drops into another titi drainage, crossing a plank bridge before rising into the sand hills. At the next junction of jeep trails at 8.7 miles, turn left and plunge through the titi into mixed hardwoods, where a series of plank bridges carries you across a cool drainage beneath tall cedars.

As the trail enters the sand hills again, stay to the left at the fork in the jeep road. Cross two jeep roads, and you can see the sun glinting on RVs in the distance. The trail skirts around the northern edge of the Camel Lake Campground, where you can see the bathhouse not far from the trail. Turn left at the "Camel Lake" sign and follow the blue blazes to the campground road. When you reach the parking area, you've hiked 9.5 miles.

Lake Loop Trail

Begin: Wright Lake
End: Wright Lake
Distance: 0.5-mile loop
Trail Difficulty: Easy
Highlights: View of lake and cypress swamps
Hazards: None
Trail Connections: Wright Lake Trail
Season: Year-round
Maps: Displayed on kiosk at trailhead
Trailhead: From the intersection of CR 379 and SR 65 in Sumatra, drive south on SR 65 for 2.5 miles. Turn right onto FR 101 (Wright Lake Road) and follow it west for 1.5 miles to the Wright Lake Recreation Area entrance on the right. Turn right and follow the entrance road up to the kiosk. Stop and pay your $3 per vehicle usage fee, then park in the large parking area overlooking the lake. Walk toward the lake and along the lakeshore to the left to find the trailhead kiosk.

Mostly encircled by cypress trees, Wright Lake is a little gem in the Apalachicola savannas south of Sumatra, with a campground that is one of the lesser used in the forest due to its distance from major highways. The Lake Loop Trail is a nature trail that circles the lake, connecting the picnic area and campground, and shows off a tiny bit of what the longer Wright Lake Trail has to offer.

Starting at the trailhead kiosk, walk past the small cypress swamp to the trail junction and turn right. Follow the combined blue and white blazes through a pine plantation on the edge of the floodplain forest surrounding Wright Lake. The trail crosses a creek on a broad boardwalk, providing a nice look at aquatic plants growing in the clear water and, in spring, at titi in bloom. At the next junction continue straight, following the trail along the ecotone between bayhead swamp and pine flatwoods. Although you can't see the lake, the trail continues to parallel the shore as it enters the campground, where you get a glimpse of blue across the campsites. The blazes are sporadic, so stay as close to the lake's edge as possible to follow the trail through the campground and around back to the beach next to the main parking area for Wright Lake.

Wright Lake Trail

Begin: Wright Lake
End: Wright Lake
Distance: 4.6-mile loop
Trail Difficulty: Moderate
Highlights: Pitcher plant savannas
Hazards: Tricky bridge crossing
Trail Connections: Lake Loop Trail
Season: Fall–spring
Maps: Displayed on kiosk at trailhead
Trailhead: From the intersection of CR 379 and SR 65 in Sumatra, drive south on SR 65 for 2.5 miles. Turn right onto FR 101 (Wright Lake Road) and follow it west for 1.5 miles to the Wright Lake Recreation Area entrance on the right. Turn right and follow the entrance road up to the kiosk. Stop and pay your $3 per vehicle usage fee, then park in the large parking area overlooking the lake. Walk toward the lake and along the lakeshore to the left to find the trailhead kiosk.

In just 4.6 miles, this trail showcases some of the best the Apalachicola National Forest has to offer. You'll see ancient longleaf pines and giant cedars, floodplain forests, depression marshes, cypress-lined creeks, and pitcher plant savannas. It is easily one of the most interesting hikes in the forest in springtime, and you will see wildlife here.

From the parking area walk down to the lake and turn left. Stop and study the information kiosk with its habitat descriptions and map. Walk down the blue-blazed path. You come to the trail junction with the Lake Loop Trail in a few moments. Continue straight through a vast open understory of longleaf pine forest. The trail rounds a pop ash–lined pond before dropping down a driveway into a campsite along cypress-lined Owl Creek, a beautiful tributary of the Apalachicola River. The trail follows the ecotone between the floodplain forest and pine plantation.

A double blue blaze marks a sharp left turn at 0.8 mile. After you pass a clearing on the left, note the unusual cedars with their whorled bark. A short spur trail leads to the swamp's edge at 1 mile. The trail swings uphill through a pine plantation, providing a brief look at alleyways of

Figure 25. Pine woods such as these harbor red-cockaded wood-pecker nests. Photo by Sandra Friend

pines as it slips around a cypress-lined pond where lilies rest on the placid surface. A sharp right turn leads you to an unusual bridge at 1.5 miles—it's like a balance beam, with a cord to help you keep your balance.

Look down and admire the clarity of Coffee Branch, but keep your footing, as it is not as shallow as it looks. On the opposite side of the marsh the trail rises up into an open forest of longleaf pine and wiregrass. Turning to the left, it parallels a forest road. Keep your eyes on the edge where wiregrass and marsh meet: clusters of colorful hooded pitcher plants grow along this boggy edge. At 1.8 miles the trail joins the road briefly to cross a creek and then veers left into the savannas to parallel the pitcher plant bogs again. In late March and early April, the many-flowered grass pink, a terrestrial orchid, blooms in profusion in these moist soils. Just before the trail crosses the road, look off to your left for spectacular displays of pitcher plants in the distant savanna.

Beyond the road the trail rises up into drier pine flatwoods. More pitcher plant bogs are in the savannas off to the left. At 2.5 miles the trail reaches a junction with a jeep road. Turn left and follow the blue blazes down the jeep road under the shade of turkey oaks and longleaf pines. A double blaze ushers the trail back into the woods on the left, and you can see some structures in the distance. After crossing another forest road at 2.8 miles, you encounter white-banded longleaf pines, nesting trees for endangered red-cockaded woodpeckers.

Crossing a broad sand road at 3.1 miles, the trail continues around a large sinkhole pond, where bracken fern creates a green haze in the surrounding understory. Cross a jeep trail and then a power line at 3.6 miles, and then the trail winds around an interesting depression with layers of texture before your eyes: saw palmetto in the foreground, pop ash just behind, and tall cypresses in the middle of the basin. Turning left onto a jeep trail, the trail soon crosses another forest road at 3.9 miles into a longleaf pine forest with a very open understory, passing more red-cockaded woodpecker nest trees before rising up into a younger pine forest. You reach a junction with the Lake Loop at a bench at 4.3 miles. To continue along the main hiking trail, turn right.

Circling a cypress pond on the right, the trail leads into a tunnel beneath the boughs of laurel oaks in the shade of the upland forest. You reach another junction with the Lake Loop; turn right to continue on the main trail, walking through more upland pine forest along the edge of a pine plantation before crossing a broad boardwalk. You can see Wright Lake off to the left. The loop ends at 4.6 miles. Turn left to pass the informational kiosk and return to the parking area.

Hiking Trails of Gulf Islands National Seashore

In northwest Florida lie several parcels of protected coastline and barrier islands. The far-flung federal composite called Gulf Islands National Seashore stretches for 150 miles in eleven sections, covering not only part of the Sunshine State's coastline but also coastal Mississippi. Individual areas encompass pristine beaches, historic forts, and rich maritime forests. For Florida hikers this means treks along sandy stretches that contrast with emerald ocean waters, through sand pine scrub and marshy inland woods, past old military installations, and beneath huge live oaks that were once slated for constructing wooden ships.

On Santa Rosa Island, a slender sandy sliver fronting Pensacola Bay and overlooking the Gulf of Mexico to the south, are two sections of the Florida Trail. Although unlike the rest of the FT, they are every bit as representative of the real Florida as are the Everglades. Here the trail traces the shoreline of the barrier island overlooking the Gulf on one side and threads through sea oats–covered sand dunes of varying sizes on the other side.

On the west end of Santa Rosa Island, the Florida Trail makes its home stretch in grand fashion. It leaves the coast and heads inland to the historic Fort Pickens, the western terminus of the entire Florida Trail. Intrepid hikers who start in the state's deep south at Big Cypress National Preserve are glad to see the brick fort that once protected the entrance to Pensacola Bay. Fort Pickens, site of Civil War activities and once quarters for Geronimo, is not the only standing artifact of military history. Steel and concrete batteries from World War II can also be seen on Santa Rosa Island.

On the mainland the Naval Live Oaks area offers woodland hiking with ocean views. This area was America's first forest preserve: the live oaks were preserved by President John Quincy Adams for use in shipbuilding for the U.S. Navy. Across this very parcel is a remnant of the old Pensacola–St. Augustine Road—the first road in Florida. Hikers can walk this old mail route as well as trails that offer overlooks of Santa Rosa Sound and Pensacola Bay.

Trail Updates at a Glance

- All nature trails on Santa Rosa Island are closed due to extensive hurricane damage

Florida Trail, Gulf Islands National Seashore

Begin: Navarre Beach
End: Fort Pickens
Distance: 13.2 miles
Trail Difficulty: Difficult
Highlights: Sugar-white sands, beach walking, emerald ocean waters, northwest terminus of Florida Trail
Hazards: Complete exposure to sun and elements
Trail Connections: None
Season: Year-round
Maps: Florida Trail Seashore
Trailhead: From the town of Navarre on US 98, head south on State Road 399 across Santa Rosa Sound to Santa Rosa Island. Keep west on 399 for 3.2 miles to Gulf Islands National Seashore.

Figure 26. Hikers travel along the Florida Trail at Gulf Islands National Seashore during the annual Panhandle Trace Hike. Photo by Sandra Friend

This section of the Florida Trail was devastated by hurricanes in 2004 and 2005. Though the trail may be walked, it is a pure beach walk with no facilities, and the western end area around Fort Pickens cannot be reached by road at the time of writing. Visit the Florida Trail website, www.floridatrail.org, to get the latest updates on this trail section.

Naval Live Oaks Visitor Center Trail Extension

Begin: Naval Live Oaks Visitor Center
End: Gulf Breeze
Distance: 1.6 miles
Trail Difficulty: Easy
Highlights: Huge live oaks, ocean views
Hazards: None
Trail Connections: Naval Live Oaks Nature Trail
Season: Fall–spring
Maps: Gulf Islands National Seashore map, GINS handout
Trailhead: From the town of Gulf Breeze, head east on US 98 for 2 miles to the Naval Live Oaks Visitor Center. The trail starts in the back of the visitor center. Look for the "Nature Trail" sign.

This path starts as the Visitor Center Nature Trail and heads to an observation deck. Most people turn around at the observation deck and return to the visitor center via two small side trails that make a figure eight. But rewards await those who continue beyond the observation deck and walk to the Gulf Islands National Seashore boundary near the town of Gulf Breeze.

The reason this section of forest is preserved involves the foresight of a long ago president, but not for reasons you may think. In 1828 John Quincy Adams authorized the purchase of this land of extraordinary live oaks for ship-building purposes. The U.S. Navy needed a good, protected source of wood to build the ships of the day. The evolution of ironclad ships soon diminished the need for wooden ships, but the property remained in government hands until it was made part of the Gulf Islands National Seashore. Today, you can travel among the oaks and look at trees that were once slated to do a little traveling themselves.

Head west from behind the visitor center. The path immediately diverges—stay left and walk over hills of live oaks draped in Spanish moss. Interpretive signs show how trees were used in the ship-building process. Pass another trail intersection and stay left, coming to an observation deck at 0.3 mile. The deck is surprisingly far above the waters of Santa Rosa Sound.

To pick up the extension of the nature trail, walk a few feet to the right past the observation deck, then make a left, once again heading west. The wrong path will soon take you to noisy US 98. Enjoy more rich woods of live oak, red cedar, hickory, and magnolia. At 0.8 mile come to a trail junction, with paths leading left to an ocean view and right to US 98. Pass over a ravine at mile 1.1. From here the bridge to Santa Rosa Island is visible. At mile 1.3 come to another junction with a trail splitting left and right—keep forward. Some of the biggest live oaks lie along the trail here.

At mile 1.6 the path dead-ends. To your left it is a short distance to a final view of Santa Rosa Sound and the ocean. To your right it is a short distance to US 98. On your return trip, make sure to complete the figure eight loop on the nature trail near the visitor center.

Beaver Pond Trail–Old Borrow Pit Trail Loop

Begin: Reservation Road
End: Reservation Road
Distance: 2.2 miles
Trail Difficulty: Moderate
Highlights: Beaver Pond
Hazards: Sun, loose sand
Trail Connections: Old Quarry Trail, Pensacola–St. Augustine Road
Season: Fall–spring
Maps: Gulf Islands National Seashore map, GINS handout
Trailhead: From the Naval Live Oaks Visitor Center, head east on US 98 for 0.7 mile to Bayshore Road. Turn left on Bayshore Road and follow it for 0.5 mile to Reservation Road. Turn left on Reservation Road and follow it for 0.5 mile to a sharp right turn. The Beaver Pond Trail starts behind the wooden gate on the left at the sharp right turn.

This hike uses three trails of the Naval Live Oaks area to form a loop that takes you through four environments: sand pine scrub, live oak forest, longleaf pinelands, and a hardwood swamp. Start by passing Beaver Pond and head south to intersect the old Pensacola–St. Augustine Road (subject of the next trail profile). Walk this path briefly, then swing north on the Old Borrow Pit Trail. Finally, pick up a footpath and walk along Beaver Pond and look down on its hardwood swamp forest.

Begin by walking around the wooden gate beneath a magnolia tree and heading south on the Beaver Pond Trail. Trace the jeep road past live oaks. Look left for Beaver Pond, then intersect a trail leading left along Beaver Pond. Keep forward, staying on the jeep road to intersect the Old Quarry Trail at 0.3 mile. Stay right, entering a longleaf pineland. The trailbed here is loose sand.

At 0.8 mile intersect the Pensacola–St. Augustine Road. Turn left and follow the old road for 0.2 mile, passing the southbound portion of the Old Borrow Pit Trail leading right, then coming to the northbound portion of the Old Borrow Pit Trail leading left. Leave the Pensacola–St.

Augustine Road and turn left on the northbound Old Borrow Pit Trail, which is marked with red tags. The path divides the forest: on your left are longleaf pines and on your right is a longleaf–sand pine mix. These trails serve as fire lines when prescribed burns are conducted, resulting in distinct habitats on one side of the trail and on the other. By the time you intersect the Old Quarry Trail at 1.4 miles, sand pines have taken over the entire forest.

Stay forward on the Old Borrow Pit Trail for 0.2 mile farther and look for a footpath leading left, marked with an orange tag. This attractive pathway swings along the margins of Beaver Pond beneath tall magnolias. Off to your right are the tupelo trees of Beaver Pond. This pond may be nearly dry at times. Come to a wide jeep track at mile 2.1 and turn right, to arrive at Reservation Road at mile 2.2.

Old Pensacola–St. Augustine Road

Begin: Bayshore Road
End: Gulf Breeze
Distance: 2.5 miles
Trail Difficulty: Moderate
Highlights: Historic road, views of Pensacola Bay
Hazards: Sun, slow walking through loose sand
Trail Connections: Beaver Pond Trail, Old Borrow Pit Trail
Season: Fall–spring
Maps: Gulf Islands National Seashore map, GINS handout
Trailhead: From Naval Live Oaks Visitor Center on US 98, head east on US 98 for 0.7 mile to Bayshore Road. Turn left on Bayshore Road and follow it just 200 feet to the trailhead, which is on your left. Parking is available on the road parallel to the trail or 0.3 mile past the trail on Bayshore Road.

This hike follows a historic road that once connected the port towns of Pensacola and St. Augustine. This federal thoroughfare, once a mail route, was built in 1824 and was the first publicly funded road in the state. You can trace this once important connector through a hilly sand pine forest, with occasional views of Pensacola Bay. The east end of the trail offers connections to other trails in the Naval Live Oaks area.

Leave civilized Bayshore Road and head west into the preserve, walking up a hill in sand pine scrub forest. Blue tags on the trees mark the trail. At 0.4 mile intersect the Old Borrow Pit Trail, which leaves to the right. Shortly after this, pass the continuation of the Old Borrow Pit Trail leading left. Stay west and intersect the Beaver Pond Trail at mile 0.6 mile. Travel through a longleaf pine and palmetto wood. The trail becomes hilly—climb a particularly big hill at 0.9 mile. Come back to sand pine scrub. A side trail leads right to a view of Pensacola Bay. Cross a paved road leading to a youth group camp and veer right, passing a picnic shelter.

Climb another hill in a live oak forest. At the top of a hill, a side trail leads right with views of Pensacola Bay. At 2.0 miles, leave the area of live oaks and enter sand pine scrub after dropping down a hill. Pass a side trail leading left 0.4 mile through sand pine scrub to US 98. The sand pines, turkey oaks, and sand live oaks sometimes form a canopy, sometimes not. In open areas the sand floor is loose. Where the canopy extends overhead, the trailbed is firmer. Continue forward on the old road and come to a wooden gate and the national seashore boundary at 2.5 miles, ending this preserved segment of the old Pensacola–St. Augustine Road.

Other Recreation Opportunities in Florida's National Forests, Parks, and Preserves

This book covers the hiking trails of Florida's national forests, parks, and preserves. Within the confines of these federal lands, other recreation opportunities exist that can complement your hiking adventures. Canoeing, fishing, swimming, mountain biking, and camping can enhance a visit to the wild wonders of Florida.

Biscayne National Park

First declared a national monument in 1968, then a national park in 1980, Biscayne is an exotic place of tropical forests and rich, colorful waters. Numerous keys running in a north-south line form the land portion of Biscayne National Park. But with over 90 percent of the park being water, aquatic activities such as saltwater fishing, boating, snorkeling, crabbing, lobstering, and diving are enjoyed. The waters of Biscayne Bay are crystal clear and a sight to behold. Two of the islands, Elliott Key and Adams Key, offer primitive camping.

Anglers vie for marlin and sailfish off the keys. Between the keys, snapper and grouper are the biggest catches. Several submerged shipwrecks, such as that of the *Arakanapka*, are diving destinations. So are the protected coral reefs. Snorkelers seek out shallower and more protected waters. Parasailers are seen in Biscayne Bay. Three of the many park keys can be explored. Elliott Key is the largest. It has a swimming area, a small harbor for docking, and a campground that over looks

Biscayne Bay. Boca Chita Key has a camping area and boat dock as well as a lighthouse. Boaters can dock at Adams Key and picnic there.

Everglades National Park

Everglades National Park is by far the largest of the federal lands included in this book. It has a correspondingly sizable range of activities. Most of them, not surprisingly, are water oriented.

On the way in, stop at the park visitor center. A museum and displays explains the web of life making up the Everglades. After this introduction, head out on a canoe, a motorboat, a sailboat, or a tour boat to explore the waterscape. A park-authorized concessionaire has various boats and canoes for rent.

Canoeists can head out on a ranger-led trip into Florida Bay. The Nine Mile Pond Trail actually travels only five miles but can be a boon for birders. Coot Bay Pond, Bear Lake Canoe Trail, and Mud Lake Noble Hammock are other paddling places. Quiet paddlers let the wildlife come to them. Saltwater anglers can fish the quiet creeks and lakes or the big water of Florida Bay. Adventurous paddlers can head into the backcountry and go on trips lasting from two days to two weeks, staying at some of the more than fifty backcountry campsites. You can also take a cruise into the backcountry, Florida Bay, or Whitewater Bay or sail into the sunset. Contact the concessionaire at Flamingo for departures and prices of these sightseeing cruises.

There are two distinctly different kinds of campgrounds accessible by car. Long Pine Key is in the park's interior. It is large but also a surprisingly quiet getaway, situated in a tall slash pine woodland beside Long Pine Key Lake. All manner of campers stay here, though it has no showers. The Flamingo area has two camping areas right on Florida Bay for your enjoyment. One is for tenters only and the other is for tent, pop-up, and RV campers. Cold water showers are available. The atmosphere at Flamingo is laid back, and everything moves at a relaxed pace, just as it should be in a campground at the end of a long dead-end road. Winter is the time to overnight here. The bugs and heat all but shut the campground down by May, after a season beginning in November. The weather in winter can be near ideal, with warm days and cool nights. Mosquitoes are certainly less of a problem than summer.

Big Cypress National Preserve

Short on development and long on natural beauty, Big Cypress National Preserve is a place where enthusiasts have to make their own good times. Some South Florida residents use swamp buggies and air boats to venture into the backcountry. Most of us are without these resources and have to enjoy the Big Cypress by more conventional means, such as auto touring, canoeing, and fishing. Most camping facilities are primitive, with the exception of a few sites.

Auto tourists find wildlife abundant in the canals alongside Tamiami Trail. Be careful if you pull off the road. Turner River Road offers a much quieter driving experience, as do Wagon Wheel Road and Janes Scenic Drive. Loop Road is a rougher gravel road that makes a 26-mile trip into the heart of the Big Cypress. Anglers are seen fishing the sloughs, creeks, and canals around Loop Road.

Two of Florida's most attractive canoe trails originate in the Big Cypress. The Halfway Creek Canoe Trail begins off Seagrape Drive, initially heading down a canal. Then things get wild as it passes through sawgrass prairies, palm stands, and mangrove tunnels before ending near the Gulf of Mexico in Everglades City. The Turner River Canoe Trail makes a longer trip on the restored Turner River through cypress swamps, open grassy plains, mangrove tunnels, and brackish ponds before passing by a high Calusa shell mound near Chokoloskee Island.

Campgrounds are abundant in the Big Cypress. Dona Drive Campground is the most developed, with a dump station for RVs but with no showers. RVs favor the other campgrounds along Tamiami Trail, such as Monument Lake, Midway, and Burns Lake. Tenters seek out the more primitive areas, such as Pinecrest and Mitchell Landing on Loop Road. These areas have no facilities and no fees. On the north side of the preserve lies Bear Island. This is a rustic hunt camp in a forest of palms and pines. Nearby are numerous trails for hikers, bikers, and off-road vehicles. More developed private campgrounds are near and at Everglades City.

Canaveral National Seashore

The North District of Canaveral National Seashore, where the hikes in this book are found, provides a popular launch point for sea kayaking expeditions on the Indian River Lagoon. Surfers revel in the big waves, especially near Castle Windy, and bicyclists make use of more than 12 miles of roads to test their stamina in the constant salt breeze. Fishing piers are at parking areas 7 and 8, and a paved boat ramp is near the visitor center. Horseback riding along the beach is permitted from November 1 through April 30 with a special permit available at the visitor center. At the Eldora Village Historic Site, there are guided tours of the old State House. Rangers lead turtle walks during sea turtle nesting months of June and July. Call in May for reservations.

The visitor center is open daily from 9:00 a.m. to 5:00 p.m. Stop in for maps, interpretive guides, and an overview of the habitats and creatures of the seashore.

Ocala National Forest

Numerous recreation activities are part of what makes the Ocala Florida's most popular national forest. Swimming, mountain biking, canoeing, and fishing can be done from several superlative campgrounds spread throughout the federal land. The springs of the Ocala—Juniper, Alexander, Silver Glen, and Salt—are nationally famous. Recreation areas lie beside these clearwater springs, where forest visitors can camp, canoe, swim, and fish. Numerous natural lakes offer other watery recreation activities.

Most of the springs have roped-off swimming areas. Folks can cool off and even snorkel in the relaxing waters. Clearwater Lake has a beach. And those who don't want to be in the water can enjoy it from a canoe. The most popular spring runs are down Juniper Creek, which flows through the Juniper Prairie Wilderness; Salt Springs Run, which flows into large Lake George; and down Alexander Springs Creek. The Ocklawaha River offers blackwater paddling down a cypress-lined swamp river. Farles Lake, Sellers Lake, and Hopkins Prairie are quiet places for stillwater exploration.

Anglers can fish Rodman Reservoir, Wildcat Lake, Lake Dorr, Clearwater Lake, Lake Eaton, and numerous other scattered waters throughout the forest. More remote lakes are plentiful too. In the southern section of the forest the Paisley Woods Bicycle Trail traverses a 22-mile circuit through the hills and around the ponds of the region.

Campers may be hard pressed to decide which campground to

choose. Nearly all the camping areas are scenically located along springs and lakes. Some of my favorites are among those listed here. Salt Springs, Juniper Springs, and Alexander Springs are the most developed and offer numerous amenities, such as hot showers. Lake Eaton and Clearwater Lake are smaller, quieter, and well-kept lakeside camps. On the more rustic side are Hopkins Prairie, Lake Delancy, and Farles Prairie. Decide the level of comfort you seek and then find your campground.

Osceola National Forest

The Osceola is Florida's smallest national forest, yet proportionally offers as much to enjoy as the larger national forests. Most of the recreation here is centered around Ocean Pond, a historic and eye-appealing body of water. A beach, boat landing, campground, and preserved Civil War battlefield are all nearby. Fishing and horseback riding round out the slate at Osceola.

Neither ocean nor pond, Ocean Pond is a bowl-shaped lake two miles in diameter. Boat ramps allow boaters to fish for largemouth bass, bluegill, or crappie. Ocean Pond is big enough to enjoy other water sports, too. Both kids and adults can enjoy the campground swimming beach and Olustee Beach on the south side of the lake.

The Olustee Battlefield is just a short drive or a longer walk from Ocean Pond. Here is the site of the battle of Olustee, the largest Civil War battle fought in Florida. Explore the small museum there and learn about the 1964 altercation. Every February a battle reenactment is held, drawing history buffs from far and wide.

A network of riding trails make horseback riding very popular. The interconnected loops near West Tower avail a total of 50 miles of equestrian paths. Besides Ocean Pond, small unnamed ponds and the Middle Prong St. Marys River offer more angling opportunities.

Ocean Pond campground is spread out along the shoreline. Tall pines tower overhead. Spanish moss hangs from the hardwoods. Grass and pine needles carpet the forest edges. Cypress trees border the water. This campground attracts a cross section of campers who enjoy a cross section of activities. It is full on summer weekends and holidays but maintains a pleasant atmosphere. Facilities include hot showers. The best primitive camps are West Tower and Hog Pen Landing.

Apalachicola National Forest

The recreation opportunities match the large size of the Apalachicola National Forest. Anglers can choose between rivers and lakes to pursue fish. This national forest is as well known for its excellent canoeing as for its section of the Florida Trail; it has two wilderness rivers, one long distance paddling river, and other smaller creeks. The Munson Hills Off-Road Bicycle Trail tackles some of Florida's most hilly terrain. Three highly recommended camping areas will keep you in the forest day and night.

The Ochlockonee River, Kennedy Creek, and Lost Creek are favorites with local fishermen. Of the natural lakes that dot the forest, try Camel Lake, Trout Pond, and Moore Lake for bass and bream. All this water is also good for canoeing. Two rivers of special note, the Sopchoppy and the New, pass through federally designated wildernesses. They are both clean blackwater rivers with sandbars of white sand and bordered by huge cypress trees that make for remote and rustic paddling experiences.

The Ochlockonee River makes both short and long distance trips viable. Various landings between Lake Talquin in the north and US 319 let paddlers choose trips of up to 60 miles in length. Most of the riverside scenery is wild national forest land. Lost Creek, near Crawfordville, makes for a much shorter trip along an intimate stream. Three feeder streams of the Apalachicola River—Kennedy Creek, Owl Creek, and River Styx—are slow-moving blackwater streams that make a there-and-back paddle through swamp habitats.

The three best campgrounds in the forest are Wright Lake, Camel Lake, and Hickory Landing. Wright Lake is the most developed, with hot showers. The twenty sites are set in a parklike pineland and have a relaxed atmosphere. Camel Lake has only six campsites on the shore of a spring-fed pond. It is quiet during the winter, but in summer swimmers come to cool off in the crystal-clear water. Hickory Landing is a small, old-fashioned national forest campground on the bank of Owl Creek. Come here if you want to get away from it all.

Gulf Islands National Seashore

All facilities at the Fort Pickens Unit of Gulf Islands National Seashore are closed due to lack of road access. Hurricanes Ivan and Dennis destroyed much of the park's infrastructure, but the historic fort and its batteries are still standing. Stay tuned for reopening dates.

Contact Information

Gulf Islands National Seashore

1801 Gulf Breeze Parkway
Gulf Breeze, FL 32561
(850) 934-2600
http://www.nps.gov/guis/

Apalachicola National Forest

http://www.fs.fed.us/r8/florida/recreation/index_apa.shtml
Apalachicola Ranger District
P.O. Box 579
Bristol, FL 32321
(850) 643-2282

Wakulla Ranger District
1773 Crawfordville Highway
Crawfordville, FL 32327
(850) 926-3561

Osceola National Forest

P.O. Box 70
Olustee, FL 32072
(904) 752-2577
http://www.fs.fed.us/r8/florida/recreation/index_osc.shtml

Ocala National Forest

http://www.fs.fed.us/r8/florida/recreation/index_oca.shtml

Seminole Ranger District
40929 State Road 19
Umatilla, FL 32784
(352) 669-3153

Lake George Ranger District
17147 East Highway 40
Silver Springs, FL 34488
(352) 625-2520

Big Cypress National Preserve

HCR 61, Box 110
Ochopee, FL 34141
(941) 695-4111
www.nps.gov/bicy/

Canaveral National Seashore

7611 South Atlantic Avenue
New Smyrna Beach, FL 32169
(321) 267-1110
http://www.nps.gov/cana/

Everglades National Park

40001 State Road 9339
Homestead, FL 33034-6733
(305) 242-7700
www.nps.gov/ever/

Biscayne National Park

9700 SW 328th Street
Homestead, FL 33033-5634
(305) 230-7275
www.nps.gov/bisc/

Volunteering

If you are interested in volunteering to keep Florida's trails in good shape
please contact:
Florida Trail Association
5415 SW 13th Street
Gainesville, FL 32608
(877) HIKE-FLA
www.floridatrail.org

A lifelong day hiker who started backpacking while living in the mountains of Pennsylvania, Ocala author Sandra Friend knows hiking well. After moving back to Florida in 1999, she began exploring the state in earnest and became enthralled with the natural beauty of Florida's outdoors. Sandra has walked more than 2,200 miles on Florida's footpaths since 2001 and has written a dozen books about Florida, including *Hiker's Guide to the Sunshine State* (UPF, 2005). This is her eighth book on Florida hiking. She is a member of the Florida Outdoor Writers Association and the Society of American Travel Writers. In addition to her extensive freelance work, which includes articles for newspapers, magazines, and Web sites, Sandra works as the communications director for the Florida Trail Association. For more information about Sandra, please visit www.sandrafriend.com. For more information on hiking in Florida, visit her Florida Hikes! Web site at www.floridahikes.com

Johnny Molloy is an outdoor writer based in Johnson City, Tennessee, who spends his winters in Florida. A native Tennessean, he was born in Memphis and moved to Knoxville in 1980 to attend the University of Tennessee. It was in the nearby Smoky Mountains that he developed his love of the natural world, which has since become the primary focus of his life.

Johnny has averaged more than a hundred nights in the wild per year since the early 1980s, backpacking and canoe camping throughout our country, in nearly every state. He has spent over 650 nights in the Smokies, where he cultivated his woodsmanship and expertise.

Today Johnny employs his love of the outdoors as an occupation. The results of his efforts are more than thirty books about hiking, camping, paddling, and true outdoor adventure, covering the southeastern United States from Florida to West Virginia and including Wisconsin and Colorado. Johnny has also written numerous articles for magazines and Web sites. He continues to write and travel extensively to all corners of the United States, following a variety of outdoor pursuits. For the latest on Johnny, please visit www.johnnymolloy.com.

Related-interest titles from University Press of Florida

30 Eco-Trips in Florida: The Best Nature Excursions (and How to Leave Only Your Footprints)
Holly Ambrose

Beach and Coastal Camping in the Southeast
Johnny Molloy

Beyond the Theme Parks: Exploring Central Florida
Benjamin D. Brotemarkle

Florida on Horseback: A Trail Rider's Guide to the South and Central Regions
Cornelia Bernard Henderson

Florida's Paved Bike Trails: An Eco-Tour Guide
Jeff Kunerth and Gretchen Kunerth

Florida Weather, 2nd Edition
Morton D. Winsberg

A Guide to the Birds of the Southeastern United States: Florida, Georgia, Alabama, and Mississippi
John H. Rappole

Guide to the Great Florida Birding Trail: East Section
Edited by Susan Cerulean and Julie A. Brashears

Hiker's Guide to the Sunshine State
Sandra Friend

Kayaking the Keys: Fifty Great Paddling Trips in Florida's Southernmost Archipelago
Kathleen Patton

Paddler's Guide to the Sunshine State
Sandy Huff

Wild Orchids of Florida with References to the Atlantic and Gulf Coastal Plains, Updated and Expanded Edition
Paul Martin Brown with drawings by Stan Folsom

For more information on these and other books, visit our website at www.upf.com.